Praise for *What the Heck Is Gestalt?* and the Work of Melisa Pearce

In *What the Heck Is Gestalt?* Melisa Pearce takes a complex topic and makes it understandable and accessible to everyone by holding the reader's attention with the nitty-gritty of Gestalt philosophy and methodology. This is a comprehensive and thoughtful exploration of Gestalt theory and practice written by a recognized expert and master practitioner. Pearce's work is reminiscent of Fritz Perls and his book *Gestalt Therapy Verbatim*. This candid examination of Gestalt seems to fulfill the author's wish to take the "now" into the "next." We are greatly inspired by this book and believe you will be too.

Jaclyn S. Manzione, MS, EGCM Cert.
and G. Thomas Manzione, PhD, PPC

Written with a deep sense of compassion and wisdom, Melisa Pearce has captured the essence of the dynamic and effective world of Gestalt in *What the Heck Is Gestalt?* Gleaning valuable insight from her years of Gestalt training and personal exploration, she experiences Gestalt as a way of life. This is an essential text for every practitioner, from the novice to the expert, who is ready to open the treasure within Gestalt.

Dr. Myra Heckenlaible-Gotto, EdD,
Gestalt Coach/Trainer/Consultant,
Founder, Crossing Life's Bridges, LLC

Melisa Pearce's ability to see people with all their fractured pieces and help them see that they are infinitely more than the sum of those pieces makes her a rare gift. Melisa has the ability to make wholeness and peace with one's self seem obviously necessary but also cooperatively attainable. But how does she do that? The framework for her approach, which combines Gestalt with her own embellishments, can be found in *What the Heck Is Gestalt?* This book provides essential tools for anyone working to help people step into their authentic selves.

Heath Kull, The Ranches

Melisa Pearce has truly embodied Gestalt and is a walking billboard for the work. *What the Heck Is Gestalt?* explains Gestalt in a way that is understandable and heartfelt. Her work and writing are both creative and powerfully direct, and her language draws you into the Gestalt perspective.

Andrea M. Hall, Whithers Whisper, LLC, EGCM Certified Practitioner, Attorney at Law

Melisa Pearce's Equine Gestalt Coaching Program taught me more about being a therapist than two years of master's level social work courses. Her wealth of knowledge, talent as a therapist, and creative teaching methods make Melisa a true expert in the field. As a fellow psychotherapist, I have witnessed Melisa facilitate lasting and profound change in the lives of her clients within a matter of minutes. Her in-depth understanding of human psychology and the experiential methods of Gestalt come from years of theoretical and applied experience that she is generous in sharing with her students and the world.

In her book *What the Heck Is Gestalt?* Melisa offers a current perspective on the practice of Gestalt and its relevance for today's clients. The importance of creative and effective interventions for therapy cannot be overstated, and this book gives readers the tools they need to discover this power modality.

Emma Cruse Rogers, EGC, LCSW-C,
Argo Counseling and Wellness

Wow! Melisa was able to take complex subject matter, Gestalt methodology, and turn it into a well-written, informative, and compelling read that I would recommend to anyone wishing to make positive changes in their life. Many times, I've wondered why I've made a particular decision or responded in a way that felt out of character for me. This book explains why it is important to look at our experiences using Gestalt methodologies to uncover our authentic selves quickly.

Carolyn P. Fitzpatrick, coauthor of *Equusology*,
Founder of The Horse Connection, LLC,
and Equine Gestalt Practitioner

As a therapist and Gestalt practitioner, I have often been asked, "What the heck is Gestalt?" Through personal and professional examples, Melisa Pearce has written a book that brings life to the abstract concepts of Gestalt. With her curiosity, presence, willingness to take risks, and ever-evolving being,

Melisa embodies Gestalt. Her students are inspired to look at their lives in ways that bring awareness and wholeness and allow them to move forward into more authentic and rich lives. Her readers will be similarly inspired.

Heather H. Kirby, Therapist, Author of Wild at Heart: Adolescents, Horses & Other Kindred Spirits

Melisa Pearce is an excellent Gestalt therapist. She received a four-hundred-hour Gestalt certification from Southwest Gestalt and Expressive Studies and has been practicing as a Gestalt therapist for over thirty years, continuing to become more skilled in the applied areas of private practice, life coaching, and directing Touched by a Horse. It has been my honor to observe her excellent skills as one of the trainers with SAGES and as a colleague these many years. In the last thirty years, Melisa has honed her skills to the extent that she has been able to present the complex precepts and basic structure of Gestalt therapy in this outstanding book, *What the Heck Is Gestalt?*

Roger Strachan, PhD, Director of Center For Creative Choice

"What the heck is Gestalt?" is a common question the Equine Gestalt Coaching Method and Gestalt Coaching Method students and certified practitioners get asked when they talk about their training and their businesses. In *What the Heck Is Gestalt?* Melisa makes the theory and practice of Gestalt accessible to the curious reader. She brings theory to life through examples in her Gestalt practice with clients, as well as through experiences in her personal life. With its practical approach, it is a must read for those who seek language and understanding when asking or answering the question "What the heck is Gestalt?"

Peggy MacArthur, Certified Transformational Presence
Coach and Owner, Birch Corner Associates LLC

As an expert on PTSD, Gestalt has been one of the most effective and transformational processes I use with veterans and active military because it goes far beyond any therapy that my veterans have previously experienced. Because of Melisa Pearce's training, I am able to fill in where talk therapies have failed our nation's heroes. Melisa's pivotal work has provided me the tools essential in healing the unprocessed trauma of those with whom I work. If you work with veterans or traumatized individuals, *What the Heck Is Gestalt?* will provide you with the context, clarity, and perfect understanding of why Gestalt works.

Nancy De Santis, EGCM, Founder of
Wisdom Way For Warriors,
offered exclusively through
Horses For Heroes Cowboy Up!

Also by Melisa Pearce

Books:

Equusology (Coauthored with Carolyn Fitzpatrick)
Eponalisa, The Fall Ride
Touched by a Horse Equine Coaching Stories,
volumes 1, 2, and 3 (Melisa Pearce, Editor)

Inspiration Cards:

Whispers from a Horse's Heart (with art by Jan Taylor)

Recordings:

Wisdom's Journey to Abundance
Wisdom's Journey to the Chakras
Wisdom's Journey to Your Personal Future

What the Heck Is Gestalt?

What the Heck Is Gestalt?

Melisa Pearce

Touched by a Horse, Inc.®
Elizabeth, CO

What the Heck is Gestalt?
Melisa Pearce

ISBN: 978-0-9905761-9-8

Published by

Touched by a Horse, Inc.
Elizabeth, CO
www.TouchedbyaHorse.com

Editing by Melanie Mulhall, Dragonheart
www.DragonheartWritingandEditing.com
Cover and book design by Nick Zelinger, NZ Graphics
www.NZGraphics.com

Cover photo by Kimberly Beer, Midnight Productions, Inc.
Illustrations by Alice Griffin, www.AliceGriffinArt.com

First Edition
Printed in the United States of America

This book is dedicated to my beloved Gestalt teachers Steven, Cindy, Darleen, Roger, Tom, and Joseph Z. And to my horses, clients, students, and coworkers who have all trusted the process.

Contents

Foreword

I've had the good fortune to work side by side with Melisa Pearce in a number of settings. We have facilitated therapeutic workshops, trainings for educators and therapists, family workshops, conference workshops, and trainings for students. Some of my favorite moments working with people have been with Melisa. We have fun, we go deep, and we love working the creative process together.

The excitement of the creative Gestalt process is akin to the excitement I feel standing at the top of a steep chute I am about to ski. With my skis hanging over the edge of the cornice, I am nervous and excited. I am totally present and aware. I have a general sense of where I am going to ski and how I am going to get down, but until I jump in, I don't really know where I am going to go. I am poised and ready, and I feel alive.

That is the feeling I have as the participants arrive for a workshop I am facilitating with Melisa. I have a general sense of the work that is needed for the group, but until we get started we cannot say where the work is going to go.

To work in this way, I have to show up fully. When I am in my best form, I enter into a flow state. I am awake, alive, present, and ready to be in contact with the clients. I have no idea what is going to happen, but I am alert.

When I work with Melisa, I am confident that she is in a similar state, and together we are able to hold a large space for the clients. We purposefully do *not* talk about the clients. We do not want our agenda for the clients to get in the way of what is "in the room." So rather than building an agenda, we joke and laugh and get rid of any agendas that we might be carrying. We have trust and faith in each other and in the creative process itself. We are confident that we are going to show up fully in the moment at the contact boundary.

Doing this kind of work requires a set of skills and some knowledge. But skills and knowledge alone will not prepare you to work in this way. You must also develop your presence and ability to show up. Just like dropping into a steep chute, once you are committed, there is no turning back. You better be 100 percent there or you are going to die. That is what the Gestalt process is all about—commitment to showing up fully in the moment at the point of contact. You don't have to be perfect in your methodology, but you have to be 100 percent present to do the work.

The best Gestalt facilitators know the work is not about them. They let go of their personal agendas, including the treatment plan, and allow the relationship between the therapist and the client (or student and teacher) to spark a natural process of healing that is inherent in each of us.

Guiding someone in this way is difficult and sometimes scary. It requires an immense amount of trust. Trust in nature. Trust in the client. Trust in the human spirit. It requires faith and belief in natural forces that are greater than the therapist's intellect. You have to truly believe that the client has the capacity to heal, grow, and learn. Your job is to invoke/provoke a process that is innate and natural and not to impose a treatment plan.

On the one hand, this makes the therapist's job easier. The therapist is off the hook. He does not have to figure it all out or feel responsible for making change happen. However, working in this way is scary and often does not make sense to the client. Trusting a process that is not in your control can be difficult. Often, people show up to do Gestalt work hoping for a specific outcome. They have an agenda. It can be difficult to move past these agendas into what is real and authentic at the moment.

It is scary for the therapist/coach as well. Your clients have hopes and expectations. We live in a world where people are expecting measurable outcomes that result from evidence-based practices. Helpers often feel like they are expected to yield a result. If you are doing your job as a Gestalt facilitator, you let all of that go and trust the process. That takes chutzpah!

Facilitating, coaching, and guiding in this way is an art form that takes time, practice, skill, and empathy to master. I remember sitting in my Gestalt training program in 1995 in the yurt in Durango, Colorado, with Darlene Benson and Roger Strachan thinking that I was in the presence of true masters. There was no way that I would ever do what they were doing.

It seemed impossible. But still, time after time, I put myself on the hot seat or worked with someone else who put themselves on the hot seat. Slowly but surely, I started to build my awareness, intuition, and ability to see foreground and background. I was able to see a person more fully and completely. I could sense the resistance, the parts of them that were in the way, and discern the polarities that they were caught in.

Gestalt is the framework and basis of this process. This book is an important and refreshing look at Gestalt. It is designed to provide the basics—the foundation of knowledge from which you can build a lifetime of practice.

I am so proud of Melisa for what she has created. Working beside her using Gestalt methodology and horses has been an honor, privilege, and thrill for me. Her training program is an opportunity to practice skills, but most importantly, it is a place to become a human being who can show up for others.

Rob Meltzer, MA, CEP, Northlight Family Service
March 2019

1

Experience Is the Teacher

Rain is softly hitting the roof of the yurt. Eight members of our weekly group are seated on the colorful floor pillows, their backs propped comfortably against the tarp walls. Marcie and I are in the center, facing each other as I guide her to move from her story, which she's telling me, to the somewhat hidden and vastly important trauma behind it.

She is speaking from reaction, not response, and telling me how nervous she becomes when her boyfriend drinks at the bar. He tells her she is overreacting.

"Does he overindulge?" I ask.

"No, not yet," she replies, "but I'm always afraid he will. I ride him pretty hard about it, and it may break us up."

Staying in contact with her, I say, "Tell me what happens for you when you are with him and he is drinking."

"It's okay, but I'm always nervous, and I just don't like it. Sometimes he gets upset about a ball game or something on the news, and when he starts telling me about it, I feel terrified."

I check to make sure she is safe and quietly inquire, "Is he bullying you or harming you in any way? Is he threatening you?"

"Oh, gosh, no. No!" she replies. "It's just that . . . well, I'm afraid he will, even though he never has in the four years we've been together."

I know some of Marcie's background and her family dynamics from previous group sessions she has attended. Her father was an alcoholic who raged violently at her mom—and sometimes at Marcie—when he was drunk. The police were called a few times, and Marcie remembers fearing he would kill her mother. He left her mother when Marcie was twelve, and Marcie felt relieved when he moved out. This part of her history is not in the forefront for her in the moment. In the moment, she is concerned about Paul, her boyfriend.

I connect the dots and ask Marcie if she is willing to look at a piece of her history. She trusts the process and agrees. Pulling a third pillow forward, I ask her to imagine that her father is sitting on the pillow. Marcie braces herself and even moves backward a few inches on her own pillow. I assure her that in this present moment, she is safe, and I back the pillow on which her imaginary father sits a foot or so away from her. Then I prompt her to tell me what her father might be wearing. She describes him in jeans and a hockey team jersey. I remind her she is safe and can tell she "sees" him sitting there.

I ask her to explore her truth about her father's drinking and the results of that. She frowns. I assist her with a stem sentence. "Marcie, say 'Dad, my truth is . . .'"

She is tentative as she begins. "Dad, my truth is . . . I hated your drinking." She takes a deep, slow breath.

"What else, Marcie? Tell him. It's okay."

"Dad, you terrified me when you had too much to drink. You got so angry, and I never knew what was going to happen."

"Keep going, Marcie. You are an advocate for that girl who lived in the angry household," I assure her.

Marcie continues, building speed and clarity for several minutes, unpacking her truth. Speaking her truth to him when she was a child would not have been safe for her. She moves on, making statements of her truth from the adult she is today.

"Truth is, Dad, you were a lousy father. You were never there for me at school or my meets. I could never have friends over because I felt so embarrassed. I was wounded by you and your abandonment. I don't respect you . . . and I got cheated."

Marcie takes her time venting all she's had stored within her for many years. When she has told it all, she sits back with a big breath.

I ask a group member to sit silently on a pillow on Marcie's other side, embodying Paul.

"Marcie, let's look at what you might now say to Paul. Your truth—not coming from the fear of that unfinished business, but from today, right now, with this understanding of how all of that with your father affected you."

"Paul," she begins, "whenever I'm with you and you're drinking, I see my father and his drinking. To be fair, in the four years we've dated, I've never seen you overdrink or be drunk. But somehow, I've been certain it would happen. I've felt frightened. I'm sorry. I'm working to see you as you and not as my dad. I want you to know that you're important to me, and I'm learning to trust. It's all wrapped up in one reality of my childhood with my dad's rage and violence. I see now that I was expecting the same outcome with you, which was unfair to you and to us.

"I'm clear that I would have a firm boundary if anyone I was with began to drink in an out of control way or was abusing alcohol. I would not choose to stay in the relationship. But I'm learning the difference between what you do and someone abusing alcohol. I'm seeing the damage within me from my childhood experiences, and I'm aware that those childhood experiences are separate from the reality I share with you."

Gestalt leads to wholeness. As a person journeys through their unfinished business, a level of self-awareness allows room for personal responsibility and a life of self-compassion. In many settings and with a creative variety of experiments, the practitioner and client explore, unabashedly, the personal operating system they are currently operating on with a goal of expanding in awareness and response to their world of relationships.

A reactive state often occurs because the situation at hand is similar to one in the client's past, which is what we refer to as *unfinished business*. This experience is referred to as existing in the *background*. This is a human state that every person has experienced at some level. Some pieces of unfinished business are from traumas and others may be created from not feeling seen or heard.

Gestalt is a non-diagnostic model that leads one to the realization that we each have both healthy and less than healthy reactions and responses to the world around us. Rather than labeling or viewing the personality as fraught with disorders, Gestalt encourages a person to fully acknowledge all the operating systems within them and ask where these systems took root in their life. Taking charge of using these operating systems to live happily and healthily or choosing not to engage in a happier life is up to the client. With full awareness and clearing up any residue from their past encounters and interactions, a person is peaceful and free to be who they really are and to select behaviors that enhance their life instead of remaining at the mercy of becoming reactionary.

It is not simple to define Gestalt, which is a German word. We will delve into the definition by discussing the key concepts, most of which can be immediately applied to your own experience of the world. While the world of therapy adopted some Gestalt techniques into the mainstream, it is the full embodiment of Gestalt as a way of life that we will be exploring here. And that is a journey to wholeness.

2

Gestalt Roots

Gestalt is a German word loosely translated to mean "wholeness." Fritz Perls, the psychoanalyst who coined the term *Gestalt therapy*, understood that we could not be truly whole if we did not know the different parts of self and their synergy in our personality. Wholeness of self in the present moment is the keystone to Gestalt.

But Gestalt is more than a form of psychotherapy. Gestalt is a way of life in which we focus on the experience of "now," referred to as *the present moment*. The therapist or coach-client relationship or the personal relationship with self are only possible when we know ourselves in the here and now. Awareness of being in the moment is essential in our relationships to our environment and with all beings. It is a humanistic, existential approach that is founded on the belief that we are born with natural resources within.

When we are born healthy in body and mind, we have the capacity to be in genuine and authentic contact with our environment and other beings. We are inherently capable of inventing and leading a satisfying and creative life.

Ideally, in the process of growing up in our family of origin, two primary needs—nurturing and protection—are met by our parents. While we are growing up and developing, something may interrupt the healthy, natural processes of growth, and we develop beliefs about ourselves and about life that do not serve us. And these beliefs often get in our way or fail to prove useful later in life. Patterns are created that cause us to feel reactive instead of fully alive and responsive. Most therapeutic approaches look to the past, the unknown, and the unknowable, forming labels and diagnoses to explain behaviors. Gestaltists take a more natural and holistic view. Looking to the present and the many parts of self within, one is seen with the totality of their life experience. Rather than being labeled sick or wrong, they are seen as having developed defenses and strategies to manage their experience. Gestaltists work with the past *only* by bringing it to the forefront of *now* to clear away unfinished business and offer a clear, present understanding.

Being fully present to our own life and the manner in which we move through it is at the center of Gestalt. It is a way that brings forth the here and now. The focus is placed on being in contact. Contact is a state in which we are fully aware of our own existence, our body, and our emotions. We are fully aware in the present moment of the breath entering and exiting our lungs, the pain in our lower back, or the breeze on our face.

In our environment, this may mean that we have heightened awareness of the temperature around us, the movement of the air, the light or darkness, the sounds of birds or office equipment, the taste in our mouth, the smell or scents surrounding us, and so on. Consciously, a full and present inventory of awareness is taken by dancing back and forth in present awareness of the environment and of our body. In our body, we begin by shifting our awareness to our lungs, filling them fully and expanding, followed by exhaling, finding the beat of our heart, feeling each vertebra as it supports our body, and feeling our feet upon the floor. This is done purposefully to engage in a conscious state of contact.

As we expand our awareness to include our present environment and our physical body, we are then able to exchange that awareness with another being because both people are in a state of contact at the same time.

When this other being is also mindful of the moment they are experiencing in their body, soul, and mind as they connect to us, we achieve contact. It is contact in the present moment with self, and then it flows back and forth with another while both remain in the here and now. It is being fully aware of the totality of that moment's exchange. We look fully into another's eyes or notice the pace of their breathing and then our own. We feel the energy between the palms of our hands as we touch or the sunlight hitting our faces as we sit across from one another. Contact is the defining place of being in the present used to bring awareness and foster true change.

Attention or notice is also given to the ways in which we may seek to interrupt or avoid contact. This becomes a significant factor when a person is working on knowing themselves and their parts. Paying attention to the ways in which we seek to avoid or interrupt contact is an important approach in working with Gestalt for self-healing.

While this approach may not seem avant-garde now, it was a big departure from the theories and methods of Sigmund Freud, the founder of psychoanalysis. In the early 1900s, analytical theory was the mode of the day, and it still influences many types of therapy. It holds the belief that if a person talks about the occurrences, traumas, and experiences of their life, they will come to a deeper understanding of themselves. In this approach, discussing and examining one's life in detail is thought to lead to an intellectual understanding that will benefit the client in changing their thoughts and, therefore, their behaviors.

A few years later, a departure from this viewpoint came onto the mental health scene. A person-centered approach, which looked at the wholeness of a person and their feelings, was viewed as being as important as exploring a person's thoughts. This was the Humanistic Movement led by Carl Jung, Carl Rogers, Abraham Maslow, and Virginia Satir.

In the 1960s, the Human Potential Movement was strong, and Gestalt theory burst onto the scene, finding its home in humanistic psychology. It was fueled by the work of two psychoanalysts, Fritz and Laura Perls, who developed the theoretical basis of Gestalt. At that time, the idea that it was important to "know thyself" was popular, and Gestalt institutes were opening in the boom to provide training for therapists, healers, and seekers of all types to explore this methodology.

When Fritz Perls first started speaking about his work and offering large public events to talk about it, he discovered that people in large groups could and would bare their souls to one another using this method. About the same time, *Be Here*

Now was a popular book from the famed guru Baba Ram Dass, who helped energize the era of self-exploration. Ram Dass's work dovetailed with the dawning of other modalities, such as Reichian therapy, Rolfing, Bioenergetics, and hypnosis, and these were often melded with consciousness programs, meditation, acupuncture, and other alternative therapies.

The 1970s continued to bring emerging and new approaches, and like Gestalt, they all continued to flourish in the Humanistic Movement. Many leaders of the movement were working to bring forth methods that did not label, diagnose, or seek intellectual understanding of self. Instead, they supported clients in fully experiencing themselves, holding that each client had inherent wisdom, allowing that it might be outside of their present awareness.

In the 1980s, short-term cognitive therapy and behavioral change or modification methods moved onto the scene. These were based in the analytical camp and were very far afield from the humanistic camp.

Financially motivated, the insurance companies jumped on these new modalities. Therapists trained in the new methods to survive in their financially driven insurance-dependent practices. As time and number of sessions won out over efficacy, the humanistic models fell out of favor with insurance companies.

A few of the basic Gestalt techniques slowly made their way into more mainstream practices. They were thought of as ways or "tools" to enhance the talk therapy practitioner's work. But they lacked the depth of understanding and the real essence of Gestalt. The concepts were misunderstood and often lacking a theoretical and practical basis. True Gestalt training became hard to find for those who sought to embody it.

There was a resurgence of interest in Gestalt in the early 2000s, and the theories that make up Gestalt therapy have been expanded to nontherapeutic applications such as organizational behavior and development in business, court mediation, and the field of coaching. It continues to be hailed as an effective human potential model and not a medical model.

Also, with the dawning of the new millennium, there began a renaissance of Gestalt institutes and practitioners who wanted to get back to the *purity* of the work itself. Clients saw recovery and health in people they knew who had found the original Gestalt route, and they were willing to pay directly for it due to its efficacy.

Today, Gestalt is done in one-on-one sessions, group sessions, and weekend immersion formats, as well as with couples, families, children, and teens. The Gestalt approach has been integral to my work as a therapist, but its influence has been more far-reaching than that. It has been integral to my life and in the larger body of my work.

The alchemy I have brought to coaching through my Gestalt perspective has allowed me to develop a model and modality that are truly effective for personal growth, healing deep trauma, and increasing healthy relationships with the self and others. And the impact of Gestalt on my personal life has been profound.

3

A Personal View of Gestalt

In addition to using Gestalt as a therapy modality, I experience it as a way of life. It is an art form and creative process that brings forth the continuous invention and reinvention of self, furthering deeper ways of seeing and understanding oneself.

Gestalt has led me to my spiritual path. It has been a spiritual way of working with my soul to fully express itself and understand my Creator. While allowing myself to fully explore and express, it has also encouraged me to remain nonjudgmental, with an exploratory viewpoint when others are expressing their views. Gestaltists tend to explore rather than define their world.

The attempt to define is intended to distill down to something useful and is often supported through pragmatism. But when we remain open to living a life through the lens of curiosity and experience, ideas may breathe, evolve, and expand.

During the years of my personal therapy work in Gestalt, I had a powerful dream that has shaped the way I've led my life for the last forty years. Growing up in Arizona desert,

I had never seen snowfall, and yet in my dream, I'm standing in a soft snowfall. An androgynous voice says to me, "Melisa, do you understand that no two snowflakes are identical?"

"Yes," I reply in wonderment.

I feel pulled in the dream to slowly bring my forefinger in front of my eyes. It is as if the androgynous spirit holds my hand there and asks, "Melisa, do you understand that no two fingerprints are identical?"

"Yes," I say again in bewilderment that this could be true with so many people on the planet. Yet, I know the truth of it.

Quietly, the voice says to me, "Melisa, this is the pathway to me."

I woke up knowing the dream was sent to me by the Source of all that is true in the universe. I was so deeply moved that I wept. And I hold the dream's message as my personal understanding to this day.

While some deconstructing of our beliefs may be useful, I remain attracted to the experience of my spiritual path and to honoring the paths of others, thanks to my Gestalt life.

Our human personality is comprised of many parts, like the formations in a kaleidoscope. I adored kaleidoscopes when I was a child, fascinated by the moving patterns magically forming with the slightest turn or shake of the scope. Each shift would form a wholly new and complete pattern for that moment in time. Each part of the self may be in a reactive state or, if healed and not plagued with unfinished business, is capable of *response* instead of reaction.

Our personality is similar to the kaleidoscope because we form and reform it in each moment, continuously expressing its current form each day and each week throughout our lifetime. At any given time, some of the parts forming the patterns that make up our personality are in our awareness, while others are not. Depending on the circumstances, moods, environmental settings, and patterns of other people with whom we interact at any precise time, the parts form into a mosaic, which casts the outcome.

Holding a higher awareness of these parts through Gestalt allows us to raise our ability to observe, and through that, to make active choices about who we are in the moment and what parts of self to activate. Although many things in life are not within our personal control, it turns out that the most important factor is totally within our personal control. Carrying the personal awareness of our many parts—their identities, operating systems, defenses, and origins—aids us in personal responsibility.

One of the missions of Gestalt is to complete a person's unfinished business, and through Gestalt, a person becomes responsive instead of reactive to their world. When we respond from an aware, whole, and fully present place, we are clear. In contrast, when we respond from a reactionary place, our interaction with others and the world often leads to regret.

On my university campus when I was in my early twenties, I saw walls and kiosks tagged with posters showing a photo of a bearded man with kind eyes: Guru Baba Ram Dass. The posters were in support of his popular "Be here now" movement. That simple yet profound statement came to guide me through my life. And now, years later, modern books on this concept still hit the best-seller list as if this age-old concept that life is happening *now* is a new topic to talk about.

In our culture, people pay meditation teachers, therapists, and yoga instructors so they can learn to become "mindful." Some even travel great distances for the opportunity to get this training. Though not experienced often enough in our busy daily lives, it is really quite simple: The moment that is authentically true most often in life is *this* moment.

As a Gestalt instructor today, I am deeply grateful for my early years as a private client doing my own personal deep process work. My family of origin was filled with violence, extreme strife, and mental illness, driving me to seek an understanding of other people and of myself. I did my Gestalt work as a client. I loved being a member in powerful weekly Gestalt groups, and I loved participating in many deep exploration process weekend retreats.

The authenticity that formed within me and that I experienced with my therapist, Gestalt group members, and profound teachers during those years helped me develop open, honest, and emotionally full relationships. This was also a formative time for me during which I earned degrees from the university and became a psychotherapist.

I was already a divorced parent when I did my own personal therapy work in my early twenties. I knew I was a person who easily attracted partners, but I failed to understand how to make a relationship that would be worth the work in the long haul. My standards were set low in selecting a life mate but set high in what I was willing to settle for or tolerate in a partner's behavior. I had one half of the equation, but I could not find the healthy balance.

But why? I had trust in God, loved the Waltons, revered my partners' families, and was a traditional—even conservative—

person on most levels. I was well educated, hardworking, and successful. I did not overspend and I was not into illegal drugs. But I had an inherent, huge reaction to the word *commitment.* It seemed to be a loaded, negative state of being, and the payoff was invisible to me.

So I continually sought out serious partners and marriage, but I was blind to what commitment really meant. I knew I wanted a family like the families my partners had, but having been raised in a home with violence, I had no earthly clue how to get there.

When I entered therapy, my Gestalt therapist set up new and novel ways for me to experience that *commitment* was a loaded word for me. The word was filled with my unfinished business, which had been created through my front row seat to my parents' highly dysfunctional, hugely abusive, and dramatic marriage. Like many, I had been replicating my parents' toxic relationship in my own relationships. To that point, I had been unable to create them in a less tragic way than the relationship I had witnessed growing up.

Had I selected a more traditional form of therapy, I might have spent years talking about my childhood and gathering a better intellectual understanding from a long, drawn out process of discussion. Through telling my story, I would have risked feeding my need for the familiar sense of drama I understood as a child.

In contrast, my Gestalt sessions were a more personal exploration, thanks to a series of creatively crafted "experiments" or "pieces of work." Often, the session seemed to have nothing to do with my inability to maintain relationships in my present life. The Gestalt therapist didn't focus on what I thought we would be working on. And my initial dialogue with the therapist at the beginning of each session *seemed* irrelevant.

Instead, the session was comprised of a series of emotional dialogues with the cast members of my family of origin. Some of it seemed abstract, about parts of myself I was only beginning to recognize. Sometimes it was with parts of others that involved concepts I held. And at yet other times, it was with people to whom I needed to express my truth in a quest to become heard.

I was finally expressing my truth, which would have risked my very life when I was a child. I felt the full glory of my anger and wept the fullness of my grief. I felt heard, as if the sick players of my childhood were finally forced to listen to me. Instead of avoiding the painful memories and pain, I was diving headlong into the pool and learning to swim.

To stop avoiding my pain and dive back in, I became a woman who was beginning to truly know herself. I became a woman who developed self-awareness and self-control. I never knew where the session or piece of work in group was going to end up. I learned not to "pre-think" about it, but to courageously step up to begin the process with no plan, surrendering to the process itself.

A completed piece, no matter how scary or difficult when it started, always led to great clarity and peace—the elusive peace I had been seeking. I felt complete, finished, and able to have normal responses to the ever-present triggers in my life.

A key benefit for me was a sense of completion. I did not feel the need to look at, discuss, or share the memories that haunted me before doing my work—even with myself. They were done, quickly and completely. And the deep pieces of work are still with me thirty-five years later. I have had no need to return to therapy to readdress anything. I have no nightmares and no triggers. I learned and completed life lessons once and for all in a few sessions, not through years of talking about it. No dwelling. No residual resentment. No confusion. Done! Done! Done!

I moved forward in an authentic way to keep discovering life and myself. I held high standards for myself on all levels. That meant saying good-bye to some old friends and relationships and setting sail in a more authentic life.

Over the course of my life, Gestalt has not been insurance against mistakes, struggle, or grief. But during those times, I know an efficient method that brings peace to me. I do my work and continue down life's trails. Today, after fifteen years with a man who is personally secure, happy, and in true partnership and marriage with me, I embrace the fullness and beauty of commitment as my haven.

My practice for thirty years has been a light in a tunnel for thousands of clients who either found confusion in talk therapy or used substances to avoid their pain. They knew they had triggers that set them off in reactive states. They had not known that they could change, swiftly and permanently.

In both of my advanced university degrees, I earned summa cum laude. But I credit my years of Gestalt training and my personal Gestalt experiences in working with clients as my most important education.

4

Becoming a Gestalt Practitioner

After a tumultuous childhood and adolescent trauma in my family of origin, I sought understanding and healing in my twenties. It was luck that I was fortunate to have a pure Gestaltist as my therapist. The sessions with Steven were incredible. In preparation for the first session, I journaled and planned all the things I wanted to tell him about my life and what had happened to me. Wasn't that therapy?

Instead, from the very first session, I understood that all planning, in fact, ran counter to the process. I was encouraged to live in that moment and follow what emerged from me organically.

There was nothing linear or chronological to my sessions, and each session was full of surprises. In addition to my private sessions, I joined a weekly group that Steven led. I truly began to understand myself. I was resolving whole chunks of my childhood abuse and teen trauma. Lively dialogues with nonexistent beings, role play, and dialogue with parts of myself were assisted. It was startling to me how completely different this was from nonstop talking about events, which is described as "talk therapy." Each session became an adventure, and I quickly felt more whole.

I was finishing up my undergraduate degree in social work at Arizona State University, and my personal Gestalt therapy was wrapping up with Steven. I had begun participating in other Gestalt process groups and retreats. As a student, I listened to lectures and experienced other forms of treatment. Through this process, I became certain that Gestalt was the correct form for my own practice. I personally knew its effectiveness and had gone on to work with other Gestaltists for my own development. I decided to begin formal training to become a Gestalt therapist.

I began my training in Phoenix in the late 1970s with trainers who were pure Gestaltists. I trained with six different trainers and did five years and 1750 hours of clinical training. Halfway through, I applied to and was chosen to be one of twelve people from around the US to personally train with Joseph Zinker in a program he was offering through the Cleveland Gestalt Institute. His unorthodox style of training meant that we would meet at various locations around the country for a week of intensive fourteen-hour days of training. His choice of locations seemed to be dependent on where he enjoyed being at that time. From Boca Raton to Cape Cod to Scottsdale, we met to experience ourselves, deepen our understanding, and practice under his supervision.

I was honored to be selected to study with Joseph Zinker, and I traveled to several locations to work with him in a group of twelve trainees and Gestalt practitioners. Sonia Nevis, a genius in Gestalt couples work, co-led with Joseph at some of the training workshops and had a profound effect on my understanding of energy fields in couples work.

Sonia was a petite woman of about five feet tall, and she had a depth of wisdom I could only hope to understand someday. She was not a person of many words, choosing instead to be direct and brief when she spoke. Throughout her teachings, Sonia expressed optimism and showed exceptional insight into relationships.

Modest about her fame, she always expressed feelings of humility about her teaching. She shared with me that she saw teaching as a deep privilege. This has greatly influenced my own experience as a teacher.

Sonia and Joseph had a mutual respect and friendship that shone through in training. Joseph was often the lead in explaining concepts to us, while Sonia seasoned his comments, here and there, with her wisdom.

Joseph had trained directly with Fritz Perls, and although there are many Gestaltists, I feel he is the most important living Gestaltist, as well as a leading psychologist. Joseph's concepts are the bridge between Gestalt's earliest formative days and today's more creative approach. Joseph worked alongside Abraham Maslow and integrated an artful, creative process into his work, which celebrates life.

Even as a very young and new therapist, when I was in the presence of Joseph, I understood that I was working with someone who loved the creative edge and was moving thought and understanding forward in the field of Gestalt. It was as if I were in the front row of history-making, and I remained aware that I was watching a true master at work.

When Joseph entered the room where we (usually about ten of us) were seated on pillows on the floor, our excitement created a soft whirring sound that moved through the room. He would literally sit in silence, peaceful and content, needing no eye contact with us, as if he were absorbing the energy field of the room. He often waited until someone shifted the agenda from being to doing and broke the silence. This silence and centering could go on for half an hour or longer. Finally, someone would say, "Joseph, I would like to work with you on something that I am aware of." Still wordless, Joseph would move to one of two pillows on the floor in the center of our circle and motion for the person to take the opposite pillow.

The student/client would begin to speak, and with keen listening on multiple levels, Joseph would find the access point that cued his curiosity to explore and challenge the person's thoughts, comments, or body energy. The "work" would begin and quickly expand into a creative experience for them both while the rest of us watched the process. As students, we were focusing to follow each juncture of the work as long as possible, and we felt some comfort if we knew where he was leading next. Most times, it seemed like magic when he found the true background of what his client needed to work on. And the way he set up the creative process was like a dance.

After the work, Joseph would lecture, breaking down the piece with his insights and clues about how he designed the creative piece. Soon it was our turn to work with clients while he sat and observed, intruding only if he could help further or redirect the piece to the highest good for the client. It was a challenging experience during which we each learned to drop our ego and self-consciousness to learn this sacred process.

While completing my master's degree, I had concurrently achieved additional training and several other certifications: typology with David Keirsey; Holotropic Breathwork; psychodrama; meditation; mandala of self; and hypnotherapy. I was dovetailing my Gestalt understanding with these other human potentiality driven methods.

Gestalt became my way of seeing the world—my way of living, not just a modality of therapy. I saw it as many things: as a body of knowledge available for all to learn, not just for therapists; as a way of choosing to live life from the present moment in a responsive mode of choice, not from a reactive place; and as a spiritual practice and a way of being here now.

Later, I joined three other talented Gestalt therapists—Dr. Roger Strachan, Darleen Benson, and Tom Beall—in forming a training program called SAGES (Southwest Association of Gestalt and Expressive Studies. We took several students through Gestalt training to enhance their practices.

I created my own private practice as a psychotherapist based on what I learned from Joseph in his in-depth training, as well as from many other fine Gestalt trainers. Years later, as I made Colorado my new home, I began training in coaching, and for a variety of reasons, I quickly made the transformation away from a standard psychotherapy practice to developing a coaching practice.

Coaching is a dynamic career, and when expressed through our Gestalt Coaching Method, it has proven to be immensely helpful to clients. Combining solid Gestalt values, techniques, and skills with a host of other influences blended in to form our particular method has proven to be a strong and effective approach.

5

Gestalt as a Coaching Modality

As the field of coaching quickly grew in the 1990s, many therapists became coaches. The basic tenets of Gestalt were a perfect fit for me as a coach because they offered a unique and highly effective form of coaching. It was thirty years later that Gestalt institutes began training the modality as coaching. Historically, the majority of legitimate training institutes offered the training to lay people and not just therapists.

In Gestalt, there is a level playing field between the coach and the client. As the practitioner assists the client in exploring parts of self or their process, it is important that the Gestaltist not be in a position of authority. The Gestalt coach brings to the session their own integrated self, with an ability to sit in true contact during the coach-client experience. Their behavior is self-aligned with their core values and a fully accessible emotional life.

This is a present-focused approach that exists in the moment. The client is encouraged to express and work from the present moment in the session. This may mean that whatever they cognitively thought about bringing to the session lifts away as the real work emerges. The coach tracks and attends to the fluctuations of both their own awareness and the awareness level of their client throughout the encounter, to be ready with an experiment when the moment emerges. This is the art of Gestalt.

The power in the work is in supporting the client to openly share the sacred space of their interior. The client experiences being truly heard and gains awareness, both newly discovered about themselves and also highlighted through the experiment. In the coach-client process, there should be no chance of confluence, because the coach is already healthy, whole, and resourceful, having cleared their own unfinished business during their training. This is key in our training, but surprisingly, it is not required at all in most schools of therapy and coaching. Gestalt ensures that the practitioner has full self-awareness and a constant clearing of life's unfinished business so they do not create unhealthy confluence.

Unhealthy confluence is akin to the facilitator seeing someone drowning while floating downstream in a river and instead of throwing them a life preserver, jumps in and begins to float and drown alongside them!

In a healthy, non-confluent session, the coach is watching two parallel processes at the same time—the client's and their own. The coach recognizes continual movement through a process of energy that remains in flow. This awareness-energy cycle allows the coach to follow the process and discover any interruptions or blocks in the flow that are not healthy for their client.

In the session, there may be energy from the client of resisting, overlapping, or even intersecting with the coach's own energy. The coach needs to carry awareness as they are scanning both the internal process of the client and the external expression of the client. The work is in expanding the client's choices and actions as they move through the exploratory piece.

As a coaching modality, this humanistic approach focuses on gaining awareness of the client's emotions and behavior without the coach interpreting them for the client. The coach listens to the foreground and allows the background of the work to appear.

This dynamic can be seen in the work I did with a client named Sallie. Sitting with Sallie as she wept in her session, I was aware that she was having a powerful reaction to what she was sharing with me. Whenever she and her husband had a disagreement, he had the pattern of taking a drive. In his anger, he chose to leave until he cooled off. The problem was that Sallie became terrified beyond belief. Each time that Bret left when they were fighting—which was not often—she was convinced he would never return or that it was the end of their relationship.

"Sallie, does he tell you he is not coming back when he leaves?" I asked. "Or does he say words that, in effect, tell you he is done and it's over?"

"No," she replied. "He just says he needs to get out of here for a while, that he needs some space to cool off."

And yet to her, it was excruciating. She would fall apart and cry or go into a panic attack.

As the Gestaltist, I listened to her words and observed her body language. I became clear that she was not responding to his behavior but experiencing a reactive state. I began to explore whether there was unfinished background.

Through answering my questions and exploring her family of origin, she recalled an early memory from before her parents' divorce. She was five and it was a rainy evening. She recalled being in her pajamas listening to her parents fighting loudly in their family room. Sadly, this was not unusual during that time period of the family. On this rainy night, however, she heard her father stomping back down the hall into their master bedroom. A few minutes later, the front door slammed. Sallie remembered looking out into the rainy night and seeing the red taillights of her father's car pulling away from the house.

She heard her mother crying, and over the next several months, her mother was depressed. Sallie did not see her father while her parents were separated, and life was irreparably changed. As Sallie grew up, life fell into a new normal, and she saw both of her parents on a fairly balanced schedule. She grew up and stopped thinking about the trauma she had experienced, but her body had not forgotten. That body memory was triggered by her husband's need for space.

I created an experiential piece of work for her to address her mom and dad and finish saying all she wished she could have said at the age of five. She allowed her voice to strengthen and told them about the fear she had felt, how unfairly she thought the separation and divorce had been handled, and how severe her panic was as a child. As she did this, she was able to clear words her body had held on to for twenty-five years.

After this work, she was able to share with her husband about her past, how it had affected her, and her feeling that she could build trust with him. She also shared her newfound understanding that his process of needing space was exactly that and not a sign of something she needed to panic over. The couple learned more about each other and even worked to find ways within their home to establish a sense of space when needed.

In 2008, when I began to offer a formal training certification program, it was important for me to offer it in the field of coaching.

There are seven main models of coaching. Some are oriented to support businesses or leadership. Others are more personal and solution-focused. The model that is a perfect fit for both Gestalt in general and my method in particular is referred to as co-active. Its basic roots spring from the tenets Gestalt held for forty years before Co-Active Coaching came on the market.

Gestalt and Co-Active Coaching use similar terminology for the basics of their approaches. Because Gestalt precedes Co-Active Coaching, we can easily see the influence it has on it. They are both whole-person focused, with the present moment at the center. They look at the "process" of the client while believing that the client is creative, resourceful, and whole. Gestalt and Co-Active Coaching evoke transformation through working on the present moment with clients and therefore share these cornerstones in the work.

I selected Co-Active Coaching as the model that best fits the coaching part of our training. Gestalt and the co-active model of coaching share a belief that clients have the answers within themselves for their unique situations, and yet the answers are presently outside of their awareness. This method assists the client in bringing their own truth into the healing and in gaining clarity.

The coaching is not designed to be solution-focused or even motivational to complete tasks. Both the Gestalt Coaching Method and the Equine Gestalt Coaching Method train the practitioner to ask better questions through creativity and empowered listening and to accomplish experiential work through Gestalt.

Coaching focuses the session fully on the client. There is no template for the session. It is a cocreative process in which the coach opens into a space of focus with the client, and together they move where the process takes them in exploration. The emphasis is on the relationship with the client instead of on tools, being a coach with all the answers, or pushing. It really comes down to being in true contact in the present moment to support the client in finding their truth.

Both Gestalt and Co-Active Coaching view and express the same basic cornerstones. They both see people as being naturally resourceful, and they both work toward achieving wholeness to find a higher understanding of self. Awareness comes from being in the present moment in the work as it unfolds, and the work yields transformation. The relationship between coach and client is honest and without hierarchy.

The Gestalt coaching session is one of process and flow. The Gestaltist pays attention and works with the client's expression, even when in minimization, such as downplaying the importance of a situation in the past. In the session, the coach will assist the client in further examination to find self-compassion instead of a pattern of minimizing the impact of the trauma or unfinished business itself. The coach will intervene when the client begins *talking about* experiences rather than feeling or experiencing them.

The Gestaltist coach brings forth the importance of celebrating a success, acknowledging fear, or handling disappointment and will consistently assist the client in experiencing their life and in finding their personal truth. They create a confidential, safe, and sacred place for the client to explore difficult emotions and learn how to express themselves in a wider range of potential emotional choices. They listen to body language, breathing, intonation, semantics, subtle linguistics, and what is expressed or withheld. Using intuition as a deep way to follow the process can be faster than logical thought and more fully understood by both client and practitioner.

Clients who have formerly been in traditional therapy are often surprised and pleased at the client-centered focus of the Gestalt coaching paradigm. Instead of talking about their life and staying in their head, they are invited and encouraged to move into the full feeling of their experiences and readdress them. They leave the session feeling truly seen and heard, not only by the facilitator but also by their own self.

6

Settings

Gestalt work can take place in a variety of settings: an office setting that has some space to work with extra chairs and body movement; a room large enough to accommodate groups where clients are often on futons or pillows on the floor to allow for relaxation, movement, and creative space; or, as with the Equine Gestalt Coaching Method, in an arena with a horse.

I have a fondness for yurts as workspace, and over the years of my practice, I have built several of them. Mine are canvas tents built on a platform about four feet off the ground. They are circular, carpeted, and filled with futons and colorful soft pillows. Latticework and windows make them cozy, private spaces with loads of room in the middle for the work.

Whether the location is an office, a yurt, or an arena, clients need to be in a setting where they can express themselves at any volume in privacy. The workspace is filled with props such as teddy bears, colorful plastic balls, Batakas Encounter Bats, and other props to assist creativity in doing the pieces of work. Clients need a place where they can cocreate with the Gestaltist a format of playacting that allows them to place the person (who is not really present) they are directing their energy towards to be close or several feet away.

In our equine program, the work takes place in a large sand-floored indoor arena within the proximity of a horse as a fellow coach. The ranch and arena settings often yield a natural sense of privacy.

Retreat settings are also popular for the work. Clients leave their homes and join the Gestaltist at a resort setting on a beach, at a secluded cabin in the woods, in the desert, in a mountain area they must hike into, at a professional retreat center, or at a luxury spa and yoga center. In our Equine Gestalt Coaching, we often select working ranches or upscale dude ranches to hold a gathering. There is no limit to settings that are conducive to the work. Appropriate settings are often near lakes with beautiful vistas, close to trails, or adjacent to other natural settings.

Being in nature opens the client to an unfamiliar place if they live in an urban area, and working in nature often assists a person in finding balance and expanding their ability to find themselves. Encountering familiar problems in an unfamiliar setting helps shed new light on situations. The physical activity required, along with being at one with the earth and nature, provide a natural rhythm for the encounter.

In my own practice, ten women join me at a cattle ranch in Montana that is comprised of thirty thousand stunning acres and owned by the sixth generation of the same family. I hold this retreat each summer and have both new and returning clients who attend. We eat together, ride every day, and sleep in cozy cabins at night. And the women book private massages with the ranch's on-site massage therapist. A Gestalt circle, comprised of the attendees, is established as a container for the work. The participants join together in a circle the first evening of the retreat and each morning and evening thereafter to round out the deep experience. This gives the attendees an opportunity to bring a piece of their history that they have carried around for far too long and leave it in the dirt when they head home.

In a more traditional office, or even a living room or basement setting, groups of eight to ten converge to process for three-hour evenings each week. These groups become quite bonded and experience a sense of safety with one another as they explore and process their work. Each week, the Gestaltist opens the group with a check-in process that allows each member to speak without interruption. In some groups, the time allowed for each person to speak is open, and in others, there is an agreed on time limit.

The Gestaltist may then invite members to step forward to do a piece of work or perhaps participate in creating a living sculpture of one member's family of origin, which then leads into the client's work. The work each week is done in the moment with no plan, structure, or agenda. The only agreements are confidentiality, day, time, and place to meet. The group serves as a container for the work, and the Gestaltist opens the container and hosts the process.

The confines of a small office in which the client sits across the desk from the Gestaltist is not conducive to Gestalt work, nor is space with poorly sound-insulated walls, because clients are encouraged to fully express themselves in real time as they may have wished to do when the events being worked on occurred.

What is important in creating a setting for Gestalt work is to find a place with ample space that provides a sense of privacy, safety, and security and then structure the setting in a way that allows for creativity and variety in accomplishing the work.

7

Contact and the Here and Now

All processes in Gestalt are based in the here and now. Every piece of work and every movement of the client sits in the quintessential concept of the importance of remaining in the present moment. It is implicit in the experiential nature of the pieces and is the phenomenological foundation for meaning to occur.

Being centered, grounded, and body-aware are important elements of this work, and while they are a part of the focus on the here and now, there is no denial that the past is important. But rather than simply focusing on the past, the Gestalt approach acknowledges the past and stipulates that what happened in the past and our memories related to those occurrences still exist in the present. The past may exist in the present through such things as nostalgia, resentment, legend, regret, dread, anger, and depression. Fostering it or bringing it to the present moment allows current meaning to be found.

As a society, we pay money to and take classes with specialists to instruct us on how to arrive at the present moment. Yoga instructors, meditation gurus, and Reiki classes assist in bringing people into the present, but in their daily lives, most people spend an amazing amount of time avoiding the present—unless and until they learn the importance of it. Time is spent in worry and anxiety about what has been in the past or will be in the future. In reality, our lives are lived in the surprise of daily life. We are living in the moment—not for it or because of it, but because life is here and now.

Often, we find ways to change our focus or react instead of respond, which means we become distracted from the present moment. When we begin to feel pain and start looking for a quick fix or solution to a problem, we have left the present moment. Remaining busy when someone is trying to connect with us is another primary way of avoiding the here and now, as are paying attention to fear of the unknown or to what we may lose and contemplating what others think of us.

I tell my students that I believe everyone should graduate from MSU: Making Stuff Up! This is a primary way we entertain ourselves to avoid experiencing the truth of our authentic thoughts and feelings in the present moment. Scenarios play out in our minds about how someone will react to something. Or we waste life force energy imagining what another person is thinking about us. We create possible outcomes based on our imaginings and formulate plans to offset them or avoid them. All of these activities represent just a few of the ways people make stuff up.

Judging, evaluating, comparing, and generalizing are all destructive patterns used to avoid the now. And of course, self-medication through vices and addictions perpetuate this pattern. When we engage in denial, avoidance, distraction, and fear of the unknown, we dance around the present and lose precious life moments of genuine aliveness and personal truth along the way.

Becoming aware of these patterns can interrupt the process and allow a person to move forward in their truth and make contact with another to discover reality firsthand.

Contact

Contact is a purposeful state of being in which one is totally in the present moment with oneself, the environment, or another being who is also fully in present-moment awareness of self. This place is key to fostering true change. In this state, we are sensing the fullness of our emotions, thoughts, body sensations, sounds, tastes, and sights being experienced in the here and now. This allows for the experience of contact.

Becoming grounded and fully present to your own body and quieting the mind are the first tenets of contact. Accomplishing those things involves focusing awareness on breathing fully in and out, finding your heartbeat, checking in with your belly, and becoming aware of movement in your vertebrae while also checking in with yourself about your emotional state and any thought patterns taking up space in the moment.

Next, operate at the contact boundary. This is when you add awareness of your environment or another being. This could be tasting a food and bringing all awareness to it on the tongue and in the mouth. Or it could be raising your awareness to the ambient temperature, a breeze, the sounds of birds, the hum of an airplane, a whinny from a horse, the feel of walking on carpet, the amount and level of light around you, or the scents surrounding you at that moment. When the contact boundary is expanded to include another being, you take in the sight, touch, breath, or even the emotional or intuitive presence of the other while each of you is fully present.

Contact is vitalizing. Contact is the purest form of being "in touch" or "getting" someone. We are centered intuitively through space when making contact.

Contact functions through seeing light waves interact with vision, hearing along the basilar membrane the vibrations of sound, smelling and tasting when chemicals or gaseous energy are present, and physical touch. These five senses are often thought of as primary, but I would add expressing or talking and movement as being functions of contact too.

A sense of excitement and full engagement are present when contact is achieved and experienced fully. But know that contact is a "charge" that may be interrupted, broken, avoided, or blocked by resistance, fear, loss of focus, or many other states of being by one or both of the beings involved.

The contact boundary is an alternating dance of awareness between self and other. The coach draws attention to their own and the other's breath, together expanding the lungs of both. Then each alternates between observing the temperature of the room and seeing the softness and color of the eyes of the other person.

The ability to make and stay in contact with someone is a basic tenet of humanity. Once it is a mastered state, it is selected as a path to happiness and feeling fully aware in the world. Through the practice of mindfulness, Gestaltists prefer to be in contact when interacting with others and may become intolerant of those who cannot stay in the present moment of contact with them.

One practice method of making contact is called I–Thou. There are many ways in which this is achieved. In our program, we practice for ten to fifteen seconds with each experience—felt, not timed. The individual moves through eight to ten alternating experiences of self and either their environment or another being. At each place or shift of attention, the person fully takes in an awareness of that station. I ask my students to practice a simple I-Thou exercise for ninety seconds several times during their day. This helps build a muscle of being mindful and "contact-full." By practicing this process, the coach can more easily achieve true contact with the client and themselves in the coaching process.

This can be done in any fluid order of awareness. For example, it may be ten seconds of bringing attention to one's breathing in and out, then shifting awareness to the sounds around them for ten seconds, then tuning in to their heartbeat for ten seconds, then shifting to the breeze on their skin, and so on.

Another practice may be with fully experiencing the moment with a foil-wrapped piece of chocolate. For ten seconds the chocolate sits on the palm of the hand and is felt there. Then it is experienced through sight for ten seconds, as the person observes the foil wrapping. Next, the person's focus shifts to the scent of the unwrapped chocolate. Then they experience the feel of unwrapping the foil. Finally, they put the chocolate piece in their mouth and allow it to melt slowly on their tongue, noting the reaction of their taste buds. Each step is experienced for ten seconds. This short ritual helps raise awareness of how many automatic things we might rush through in our lives without fully taking in the moment. Slowing down and coming into contact with our world allows for a more full life experience.

Once a person understands how to practice contact, they may move to doing so with another person or an animal, becoming aware in their senses of their own self for ten seconds and then taking in what they notice in connection to the other. Contact leads to awareness, appreciation, and intimacy that deepens connection.

Contact is a way of experiencing and developing relationships that are authentic in the present moment. Gestalt work with contact promotes these as daily habits. Both practitioners and clients experience the value of slowing their energy down and moving through life in an honest way that does not create further unfinished business. And the vitality—both personal and in relationship with another—that is an inherent byproduct of doing contact work is so life-affirming, it supports living in contact on an ongoing basis.

8

Awareness and Authenticity

The Gestaltist frequently asks, "What are you aware of?" The client may have to move away from the ongoing flow of the communication and turn their attention inward to identify the answer to that question and thus enhance their knowledge or wisdom of self through awareness. They may become overly self-conscious for a time.

Sitting across from Greg, I listened carefully to the content of his story as well as to the pauses he was making as he told it. I noticed that his breathing became slightly more rapid as my questions began to drill down into his story. I noticed his use of the word *it* when sharing about his father hitting him. Saying "It was horrifying" helped him keep the story removed from himself by at least a layer. I felt into my own body's empathic response and felt my calm heart quicken, knowing it was not my heartbeat but a reflection of his. And I further watched as his foot, which was across his knee, began shaking up and down rapidly as he shared.

After a few moments of listening, I found the background for the work and began by asking him to convert his use of the word *it* to saying, "My truth is, my father was horrifying when he was angry."

"What are you aware of?" I then asked.

He replied, "My heart is racing as if he were here."

"Stay with it," I said softly. "What else are you aware of?"

"I'm aware that he still scares me."

"What else?"

He closed his eyes and allowed the feeling to sweep over him. "I'm aware . . . that it's not right! It's wrong!"

"Greg, take the *it* away from the sentence Who is not right? Who is wrong?"

"My dad," he states. "I've never told him that!"

"Say it again, and straight to him, as if he were right here in this room."

"Dad you are *wrong*!"

"Good, Greg. Feel your foot shaking on your knee?" The foot stops. "Bring your awareness to your foot and shake it again." He begins shaking his foot again. "Greg, keep shaking your foot. Allow it to move faster and stronger." His foot moves as suggested. "Good. Good, Greg." And as the work builds, I say in encouragement, "Give your foot a voice!"

Greg leaps to his feet. "Dad, you are so wrong. Hitting me was wrong. Not a little, Dad, but *totally wrong*. You abused your own son!" He kicks the air with his foot. "I wanted to kick you when you were hitting on me!"

The piece of work continues until Greg is spent and peace fills his body. He has said the truth bottled up in him since he was a small child. We continue the authentic sharing with awareness. There is no need now for his body to cover over his emotions or truth.

The awareness the Gestaltist is concerned with is that which restores unity in the client's total and integrated functioning. Before being able to make effective change, the client must recover an awareness of their sensations and the feelings that accompany them. Clients become better aware through different exercises and pieces of work. The coach's sensitive guidance highlights the details of the sensations and feelings for the client to *bring into* awareness and *increase* in awareness. These sensations and feelings may have been unseen, ignored, or out of the client's awareness field before the work.

Living authentically and expressing the true self are rare qualities. Among other things, they require accepting our deep feelings and the octaves our emotions play. They also require accepting our internal parts of self. This is what being real is all about, and it is a journey well worth taking. No one can live your life for you, nor can you live theirs. Life is our precious gift, and how we express ourselves is as unique as our fingerprint when living in authenticity.

Showing where we are vulnerable and leaking clues to where we are not yet whole are parts of the challenge of "becoming." With Gestalt, we are challenged to live in tune and fully with our genuine self. Gestalt encourages us to be more direct and truthful with ourselves and others. It encourages us to live in congruence, balance, and awareness of our body energies and in harmony with our environment and other beings.

A part of achieving authenticity is knowing ourselves with heightened awareness. A goal is to recognize our true feelings and emotions, which may be seen through our actions and behaviors, and to notice when our physiology shifts, limiting beliefs are surfacing, and when we recognize we are in a reactive state to someone. It is also carrying awareness as to which part of self is actually in control and calling forth other parts in alliance so we can make choices instead of being at the mercy of emotions and actions that come forth without thought.

This is foundational to our being and moving through life in congruence. Congruence occurs when the mind, gut, and heart are all expressed in balance and harmony through words, thoughts, and energy field. What a person thinks in their mind or has a gut feeling about is expressed through their heart field as emotions. When all of these centers of energy are in a similar flow, a person is in congruence and in authenticity. Authenticity is the final and most real personal level of awareness.

Some people are more in tune with their ability to sense if someone is in congruence than others. For instance, a detective may be able to feel if the person they are interviewing is telling the truth. Other people just have a feeling that something is "off" with another person when observing how they are acting or expressing themselves. In our equine work, the horses act as what I refer to as "Equi-Detectors," because they easily feel if a person is in congruence or not. And they only move closer into a trusting partnership with the person when that person is congruent.

In life, a person has gone through whatever unique experiences they have encountered. Something said cruelly to them one time may repeat back to them in their mind thousands of times, crushing their belief in themselves—or worse. Not living in their authentic self with awareness of all that has happened and how it has affected them, they live in automatic thinking. This unfinished business can be cleared quickly and lead to a life of peace.

9

Unfinished Business

Many things in life can lead to unfinished business, which involves life experiences that have not been adequately processed, integrated, or resolved and are therefore incomplete. Often, these experiences have been suppressed and are outside the person's awareness. Yet when something is experienced that is similar to or reminiscent of the experience in the past that is unfinished, the person reacts to it instead of responding to it.

Unfinished business is sometimes a carryover from problematic childhood experiences. A six-year-old child is molested by her uncle, who comes into her room at night, violates her trust, and intimidates her into silence. She swallows her fear and experiences a loss of power. When she is an adult, she may not even remember the experience because she has repressed it, but she may have difficulty experiencing intimate relationships with men because of the unfinished business related to her molestation as a child.

But childhood experiences that create unfinished business can be far less obviously traumatic than that. For example, a child whose best friend moves away without their having had the opportunity to say good-bye might have unfinished business in adulthood as a result of that experience.

Unfinished business can also result from adult experiences. A man who has survived a car crash that was immediately fatal to his wife and son will have had no opportunity to say good-bye, express his love, or vocalize regrets. This can cause unfinished business for him. Likewise, in today's corporate world, where layoffs are sometimes handled ungracefully, a loyal twenty-year employee who is let go because of downsizing may be escorted out of the building by security. He has probably had no forewarning and no civil conversation in which the employer has expressed gratitude for his good work over many years. Neither the employer nor the employee has had the opportunity to express how they feel about the situation. That experience becomes unfinished business if it goes unprocessed.

People move on in life and mistakenly think that because they survived a traumatic incident and life has moved forward, it does not matter. But it *does* matter. Unfinished business is common, and almost everyone has pieces of it in their psyche. Some experiences are more traumatic than others, but all have a lasting effect. Those lasting effects are held in each cell of the physical body, and they may be the result of holding an unexpressed scream, repressing words or gestures, or otherwise suppressing some expression. This may cause illness, and it almost always causes the subconscious to do its work through dreams and other "nonsensical" routes to process the occurrence and make sense of it.

Eventually, triggers appear to assist the process of release. Almost as if priming the pump, when a person resembles someone who was involved in the original occurrence, a physical surrounding is similar to that in the original experience, or the situation or dynamic is similar, the subconscious begins to cue the body's emotional field. The cells begin to regurgitate the experience with emotion, and the person often finds themself in a reactive state, which is frequently misunderstood. All of this is almost always outside of their awareness, as is the reason for their feeling so strongly about the present situation. People may accuse them of overreacting, and the reactive person is left wondering why it bothers them so much.

So what happens if such a person comes to a Gestaltist for help?

When a client shows up for a session, they are often nervous and may have been chewing on what they want to discuss in the session. This may occur during their drive to the session or have been going on for hours or even days before the session.

As the time together begins and contact is established, they settle into the session and may begin to tune in and share. Often, they do this with a story or a description of events in their current life. It may be associated to a part of their life that is presently in conflict or feels unsettled. This lies in what we refer to as the foreground. In the foreground, the client may be experiencing being triggered by a current person or situation. They find themselves in a reactive state, and they may have been told they are overreacting.

Reactive states are those in which the client feels they are not in control. Their emotions or even words and actions feel almost out-of-body. This can be contrasted to being in a responsive state. When responsive, the person is aware of their thoughts and emotions and can make choices during the active encounter. This is much preferred for good emotional health.

Let's look at an example.

A manager of a large company sent one of his key employees, Sue, to me for a session. He hated to lose her on his work team, and she felt she might need to quit. At the start of the session, Sue described that when she worked with her coworkers on projects, they would be in the company's boardroom with a large table and about eight people working in a think tank. One coworker, Bill, was a tall man, and whenever he was thinking out loud, he stood up and walked about the room. Often, he became worked up and spoke loudly when putting his ideas across, and if he became frustrated, he would slam his tablet down on the table. Sue would become shaky and often left the room nauseous. She did not understand why because Bill was someone she considered a friend who had never been threatening in any way. Her coworkers told her she was overreacting, and her boss sent her to me.

For me, the red flag was that this was foreground and that she, in fact, had background to work through. The clue was that she felt she was having a big reaction to something that did not make sense to her. I began to explore with her to see if she could uncover something in her background. During the indirect process used for that, she suddenly exclaimed, "Oh, my!"

I asked her what she was remembering, and she went through a time when she was four years old and her older brother and sisters were at the family dining table. She was at the far end of the table, opposite from her father and older brother. When something was exchanged between her father and brother, they both stood up suddenly—with raised voices. Her father slammed his napkin down on the table and kicked her brother out of the house. Everyone at the table was upset, and she was sent to her room, told she was too young to stay while they talked about it as a family. The next day, her brother joined the Army, and she never saw him again.

With that information, I created a scenario so she could reexperience the situation. I set it up with a table and chairs and put two large teddy bears in the chairs at the far end. I then asked her to close her eyes and come back to that dining room. What had her little inner child wanted to say that night? I worked with her to let it all out. "Don't fight! You're scaring me," she said. Looking at the teddy bear representing her brother, she said, "I love you and don't want you to leave." To her father she said, "Daddy, don't make him go!" And to both of them, she screamed, "Stop it! Stop it! Stop it, both of you!"

Sue was tired at the end of the piece of work. She had released it all from the depths of her inner self. Feelings she did not know she held and emotions that were unexpressed had flooded out.

The next day, she returned to work and asked to speak to Bill. She explained it all to him, and he said he understood and that his own wife sometimes told him to settle down. They laughed, and the next time Bill found his passion, it did not feel like a big deal to Sue at all. He only seemed to be making his points. It was all in balance, and she was seeing the situation as it really was. She was now in a responsive state instead of a reactive one.

In the case of Sue and Bill, the foreground was presented as her becoming upset by Bill's actions at work. The background was her experience at the family dining table when she was four and there was a fight. This background was outside her awareness, and through the Gestalt process, the healing occurred by completing the background.

As we can see from this example, Sue's reactive state was caused by an experience in the background from her childhood. And that incomplete, unprocessed experience created unfinished business. This is a human state and one that every person has experienced at some level. Some pieces of unfinished business are from traumas and others may be created from not feeling seen or heard.

Unfinished business is created when a person is unable to express or control a situation that is traumatic or damaging for them. This may be due to their young age, when they are preverbal or their childlike way of expressing themselves is not heard. It may be due to a lack of safety or being dominated in a traumatic event. It could happen when a person is overpowered in an office firing. Shame is often a byproduct of this dynamic.

Some unfinished business relates to things the person reexperiences (flashback) or remembers during their daily routine or in nightmares. Others are connected to times that have been pushed so far down in their awareness that the person doesn't think about them at all. In fact, they are surprised that these experiences are seen as bothersome by the coach. But the client exhibits big reactions to similar situations that arise and brings those topics to the session. They are reactionary, and that means that they might over-involve themselves or have a larger-than-life reaction to a lesser stimulus. Even the client is baffled about how they feel so triggered.

Let's look at another example.

During a session with a close and committed couple, one of the partners, Cindy, expressed that she felt smothered. Her partner, Mary, had a tendency to "over care" for her, making her feel helpless. She felt that Mary did not trust her to care for herself in the simplest of tasks, such as making her own lunch if Mary was going to be away for the day. This was in direct contrast to reality because Cindy was well employed and was a highly responsible adult.

Mary was unsure why she felt so compelled to micro-manage every detail of Cindy's life. She was aware that it was her love style and shared that it had been a problem in other relationships.

A week later in a group session, Mary took the hot seat and we began to explore the possible background of where she first learned what it meant to care for others. As we built the creative piece of work, Mary described her mother as an absent, men-obsessed alcoholic who was interested only in the latest man in her life, her drinks, and her cigarettes. She was usually asleep. When awake, she was on the phone and detached from any responsibility for raising the five children. Mary described her as lacking the "mom tools."

Mary was the oldest sibling, and by the time she was seven, she felt responsible for the total care and feeding of the babies. She expressed her hopelessness in that it felt there was no one else to do it. Like a boxcar child, she was changing diapers, getting them fed, drying their tears, and getting some off to school. Each school day, she hesitated leaving for school out of fear that her two youngest siblings would be neglected until she returned home from school at 3:00 p.m.

This was an extreme situation, and as the piece of work was played out, I had each character begin to cry, whine, and demand what they needed from her while another group member sitting in as Mom was portraying smoking a cigarette, drinking, and laughing on the phone with a man.

We heightened the replay experience, and Mary snapped into her caring for her siblings. She never lost her temper. Instead, she focused on meeting all four kids' demands and needs at once. I watched her and began to speak in her ear as she was meeting their unending demands. "Mary, you are seven! Mary, you are a child! Mary, you just learned your takeaways in math."

I continued to heighten the experience until she finally broke with a long release of overwhelm. She shed tears and expressed both sadness and compassion for her seven-year-old self. The sadness eased up after several minutes. She slowly looked up at her mom and began to speak her truth on her own behalf.

That day in that piece of work, Mary cleared forty-five years of anger and pain. What she wanted, needed, and should have been able to express to her mother when she was seven finally flowed out of her cells and subconscious. She released and released and released, finally finding peace as the Gestalt piece of work was completed.

Mary was able to return home with a totally new awareness of her tendency to over-care and an ability to make solid changes in her relationship with Cindy.

When incidents and events are unresolved, a person is often unable to allow the memory to fade into the background of consciousness. This is because the base needs the incident represents have not been met. This unfinished business is most often outside the client's awareness, even when the situation that resembles that unresolved experience presents itself and they react. In Gestalt work, one goal is to discover these unresolved places in the client's life, including the people connected with the unfinished issue, and bring them to completeness.

Remember the work with Marcie described in the opening pages of this book? When she began working with me and spoke about what the issue was for her, that was the foreground or current story, which was fueled by the unfinished business in the background. My job as coach was to find and identify the background as the seat of the work needed by her. It was a process of connecting the dots for her. Marcie's nervousness when her boyfriend drank was in the foreground. But it was fueled by her unfinished business in the background—her father's problem drinking and her fear of him when he drank.

Once the background reveals itself, the coach may then create an experiment for the client to work with. For instance, the coach might have the client imagine a key person in their unfinished business and then assist them to role-play or do empty chair work with that person. This is what I did with Marcie. The client is given stem sentences or tools in the work to voice and interact in a safe, supported environment. In Marcie's case, I gave her *Dad, my truth is* . . . as one stem sentence.

Expressing what they were not mature enough or safe enough to express at the time of the real event can free up things felt and thought for decades, creating a sense of completion and peace. When Marcie had completed venting and expressing with her surrogate father, I then gave her stem sentences to complete with a surrogate for her boyfriend, Paul. When the piece of work is whole and complete, there is resolution for the client, and this is what Marcie experienced in her work. When a similar situation that was formerly a trigger next presents itself, the client is no longer triggered or reactionary. Instead, they can remain responsive and appropriate to the reality of the present moment.

Now that we have the framework of foreground, background, unfinished business, and a bit of structure for doing the work, let's dig into the process a little deeper.

10

The Work

In Gestalt, we speak of the work as a "piece of work." This occurs when the client accepts or initiates the invitation to sit on what is often referred to as the hot seat. The client steps into the coach's field of focus to further explore their process. This is not a small thing. The person in the hot seat is making themselves open and vulnerable to experiencing and working with things that are very close to the bone: significant, uncomfortable, and deep within the psyche. There they move into contact in the present moment with the coach. Together they begin to explore something that is up for the client—or something that comes up for the coach in relation to the client—as they fully engage in contact.

Often, as the coach employs deep listening when the group is checking in and sharing, a piece of work emerges in clarity for the coach, even though the client may not hold that realization from their check-in. Alternatively, the client may know they are willing to work or that they have a physical sensation in their body they want to explore. Either way, the coach and client engage in coming into contact to open a piece of work together.

How does the client in a group know it is their time to work? Gestalt is always an invitation to explore. Part of the work begins when the coach extends an invitation for someone to work and that invitation is accepted. There is an alliance between the client and practitioner that creates safety, which is a critical aspect of the process.

As described and shown through examples earlier, the client often begins with a story that is usually in the foreground of their awareness. As they explore this, the background begins to emerge, and the coach begins to see an experiential way for the client to explore it. This becomes the client's piece of work.

And at the beginning of a group session, the Gestaltist may simply state, "I am here and present for whoever wants to come forward to explore." The invitation may come from something the Gestaltist observes. "Brad, I have observed you going inward to process about something occurring in our sessions. When you do that, where are you?"

At another point, the Gestaltist may observe that a client in group has been triggered by a previous piece done by another member of the group and may support them by extending an invitation. "Would you like to come forward and explore how that has touched or triggered you?"

In a private session, there is an assumption that the client is looking for an opportunity to explore and work. The Gestaltist may still set up an invitation when the experimental phase of the session begins, checking in again with the client to receive permission to further deepen their exploration. This creates more willingness in the client to participate in the process.

In an ongoing group, if a client declines the invitation or stops themselves from stepping into the hot seat, a part of them knows they missed an opportunity. As they watch the work of others, a growing nudge may form in their body somatics that underscores that they're missing out. Over that session, or over a few, the client builds their own awareness, and the fact that they are not pushed to work becomes a part of their healing process in itself. Clients often seek an opportunity to have the hot seat because there is usually a limit of time on the group process. Weekly groups usually consist of six to ten participants and last for three hours. Intensive weekends extend opportunity over a period of three or four days and attract those who wish to have more opportunity for growth.

As a coach stays present and aware of all group members, they may privately nudge a resistant client, an introvert, or someone simply unsure to seize the day. The coach never pushes, insists, or embarrasses them, since their work may be held in the very process of learning to step into the opportunity.

There are clear signals to the choice. The client may experience one or more of the following:

1. There may be a topic that they intellectually know they wish to explore.

2. They may have been triggered by another piece of work they witnessed.

3. They may feel a somatic or sensation from being in a state of implosion because the body often signals disruption first. Nausea, headache, or a racing heart

are all signs of implosion. They have become triggered by an incident in which they became reactive instead of responsive or by watching another group member's piece of work.

4. As they become more comfortable with the process, they may show up with an awareness of how the process works and step up in an open and willing way to explore what may arise when sitting in contact.

5. They desire to find the meaning of a troubling dream or nightmare or even a fragment of one.

Gestaltists encourage and create a pathway for their clients to explore and express the deepest of feelings. Memories become locked in the body's cells and affect the body's organs. Grief, rage, fear, and even laughter contain emotions, feelings, and energy. The residual effect of them is housed in the brain through the subconscious, and many scientists believe they are also coded in our cells in the form of cellular memory.

To become free and whole, our bodies need to release the pent up emotions and experiences that are locked in and may even permeate the cells. Gestalt process encourages the release through tears, voice, a primal scream, or beating on a cube with a racket. Once fully heard and fully expressed, a liberation from what has been stored in memory is achieved. The person is now able to fully experience the authentic self and relax into the present moment, thanks to their having finished the work, which is a major key to their health.

As a Gestaltist for over thirty-five years, I have observed how many parenting, teaching, and even religious practices encourage people to diminish their feelings. The pattern of bypassing genuine feelings to fit in, be strong, or be what others consider appropriate leads to devastating results. This fosters superficiality and results in a person being inauthentic and out of touch with themselves. It is a large sacrifice for the sake of fitting in. In contrast, Gestalt teaches us to be more of who we are—feeling more, expressing more, experiencing more. It supports our recognizing the synchronicity in our daily lives and tapping in to our intuition.

To make that which is fragmented whole, Gestalt practitioners are trained to sit and remain open in the presence of deep emotions, including raw pain, confusion, anger, and rage. They are practiced in suspending all judgment and making room for the honest expression of what each person is holding in their body. And they facilitate a safe, full, soul-bearing release.

I encourage coaches to envision that every cell has a brain of its own within it. Trauma is remembered by every individual cell. As cells die off, new cells are produced, and the damage held within continues to transfer to the new cells until the unfinished business is completed. Each cell is infused with memory, which the body holds on to. Our health is deeply affected by the holding process in both the mind and the body.

Deep feelings are an essential part of our aliveness and our genuine experience of self. They are part of being human and not a sign of weakness or something being wrong. Our deepest feelings are not something to merely "get over." They are the real experience of being alive. Being alive and in our authentic, aware self leads to playing the full range of octaves on life's keyboard, not just one or two. To experience and express passion, rage, hurt, joy, disgust, grief, and anger allows for new insights that can take the place of the markers previously held within the cells.

What occurs is a rewiring of sorts that allows us to embrace what is and move on in life in wholeness. These genuine emotions are not born in neuroses, and it is important to understand the difference with those that are. Emotions based on fear and neurotic feelings—such as envy, feeling silly or ashamed, self-consciousness, and jealousy—have to do with self-expectation and the expectations of others, which create worry and neurotic thoughts.

As a person comes into awareness and acceptance of their true self, they may more easily drop away any excessive and irrational anxiety or obsession. Irrational expectations are often adopted from the expectations of those the person sees as being authority figures. The work empowers them to become their own authority instead of allowing others to set rules and values for their life.

There are many methods for assisting a client to release old pent up emotions through experiences that allow the space for the client to drop out of their logical, thinking mind and into their expressive body. Sometimes when I am working with a client who is reliving a painful story that we acknowledge is unfinished, the client loses the ability to find words deep enough to express the fullness of their pain. I will place my hand on their midriff and ask them to release the sound locked within them. At first, they may need to let go of concern over what it may sound like or look like. With support, contact, and encouragement, the sound takes on a life of its own. It has been entrapped in the body for years, looking for a way to escape. Through digestive issues, eczema, or displaced anger, it has usually expressed that it wants out!

We give the sound a pathway that may end up as a primal scream issuing from the deep belly of a body that is fully bent over. This usually happens a few times until the client feels a sense of completion. As a coach and empathic person, I can feel the body energy release, and I love to watch the freedom and joy the client feels immediately after doing the work.

For other pieces of work, the client may give a clue that helps set up the experience through what they express. If the client says, "I wish I could just tear you up!" I may hand them a ream of computer paper and say, "Start tearing!" As they tear, they cry. While they rip, rip, and rip, they're allowing for release through the action of ripping the paper. For another, release may come from something they write, letting the pen go crazily back-and-forth several times, like a child does with crayons when they're expressing anger. A pool floaty can be helpful when a client describes with their hands how angry they are. A floaty is a hard thing to strangle, and squeezing it with the hands, along with a sound or scream, provides a wonderful release.

For my work with clients and students, I have a large foam cube that a client can stand in front of wearing gloves and holding a tennis racket. Each whack on the cube (done properly) with sound and contact creates a loud and full body release. And when placed against a wall with the client on the floor on their back, the cube also becomes a satisfying kick platform.

This is about allowing the body to take over and allowing the mind to suspend thinking long enough for the entrapment of pain in the body to finally come up and out, once and for all. It is important for the coach to be fully trained in this approach to allow for client safety, both biomechanically and emotionally. Facilitated by a professional with experience and done correctly, this is an experience that creates peace and freedom for the client when completed.

The work emerges from the creative process of the Gestaltist. The coach discovers the background, assesses the level of complexity the client may be able to handle based on their previous Gestalt work, and then designs an experiment that allows the client to complete the unfinished experiences of their life. It is always unique, always customized, and also mutable, allowing for the highest outcome for the client.

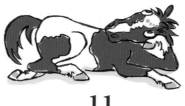

11

Resistance from a Gestalt Perspective

Resistances—sometimes referred to as defenses—are viewed differently by the Gestaltist than in many mainstream therapy approaches. Preferring not to be a diagnostic model, Gestalt holds this idea as simply a part of the client self that may be outside of their awareness. When out of awareness, these parts often do not serve the person well in developing or maintaining relationships.

The resistances are therefore in need of exploration. Finding the origination or the seed of the resistance can be helpful to the client. Noting when and where the pattern emerges in their life also yields greater understanding. These discoveries allow the client personal control as they begin to understand where they came from, how the parts of the self come together, and what they manifest. In Gestalt, the goal is awareness, not extinction of the resistance.

These resistances occur in our daily lives as well as in the therapeutic process. For our purposes here, we will explore them primarily in the coach-client experience. Below are a few of the most common forms of resistance with a brief definition and discussion of each one.

Introjection

Introjects form when a person in an authority or power position makes a declarative statement about another person's being, or process. This can be a parent, partner, spouse, teacher, minister, boss, or therapist. When the statement is made by the more powerful person about who the person being commented on is, the person receiving the comment takes it in as absolute truth instead of assessing the accuracy of the statement.

A young child, for instance, may not have a frame of reference to discount or deny whatever abusive statement their parent makes, and they accept it as truth. The introject becomes a rotting seed of self-limiting beliefs that tears away at the person's ability to see themselves clearly. This erodes their self-esteem, and it can hold them in an unjust and mistaken view of themselves.

When a person is in an introjected state, it is often due to thoughts that formed during the experience that created the introject. This happens when someone held as an authority figure (parent, boss, clergy, teacher) makes a statement about the character of a person in a lower power position or refers to some part of that person's self, and that statement is spoken as if it is a matter of truth instead of an opinion. This often results in becoming an undigested attitude in the person who has heard the statement made about them.

Ways of acting, feeling, and evaluating, as well as self-judgment, are set in place around the introjected state. This commonly happens in young children before the age of eight, because they see their caretakers or parents as more knowing than they are, and they are fully dependent upon them. They have no comparative information. Therefore, if the parent or other rule-giver refers to them as dumb or clumsy, the child takes on that identity as truth.

These undiscerned pieces of the whole, which the person has never tried on, chewed, or tasted before swallowing as truth or analyzed before taking into their psychological system, form limiting beliefs and the "shoulds" in the client's makeup. As the client does their work in an attempt to find their true self in integrity, they must take these limiting beliefs out and critically assess the undigested material. The beliefs act as foreign bodies using them as a host. Introjects lie heavily on the person, creating limits and parts of identity they did not choose for themselves.

In many cases, the introjected beliefs form blocks of energy around the stomach. This undigested foreign material is not healthy and does not belong in the person. Symptoms include issues with their stomachs and digestive systems.

Introjects prevent the person from developing their own personality and living in authenticity. Often, a person with introjects will express a feeling of not knowing who they really are. They exhaust their energy by stuffing down and holding on to the introjects they have swallowed whole. The introjects are taking up space and preventing them from clearly seeing who they really are. The more introjects the person has taken on, the less space they have to express or even discover their personal truth.

Introjects contribute to concepts or limiting beliefs that can tear at the fabric of the person's self-esteem and blur their self-perception. Anxiety or disruption occurs as they try to reconcile for themselves the truth of who they really are—not what they have been told—because the person often has no awareness of what is upsetting them.

The client's language is often full of "should," and their boundary with the world is usually a fortress or wall deep within themselves when they relate to others. The examining and extraction of introjects must occur for healing to take place.

Identifying the client's areas of self-contempt, limiting beliefs, and the "shoulds" and "oughts" they hold form an excellent start when done through creative Gestalt experimentation, as opposed to just talking about them in rational discussion. This process allows the client to redefine who they are and release their limits, giving the ill-fitting messages back to the person or persons who sent them in the first place.

Projection

There are two formats that projection operates within. They are similar yet different from each other in a distinct way. One occurs when a person is seeing another person through a veil of behavior that has been triggered but is not wholly present at the time. When a person projects, they are taking a perception that is internal and placing it on a person or situation outside of themselves.

This occurs from a person's unfinished business with someone in their past, the understanding of which is not complete. It becomes available to be cast upon another person who resembles or triggers the unfinished work in the present interaction.

Like a movie projector, the person who has triggered the client becomes a flat, non-persona screen upon which the unresolved feelings and misunderstandings are cast as an overlay. This overlay seems real to the person who is projecting because they are often in an almost altered state of emotions. And the projection may begin to sound strange, crazy, or unfit as a response to the receiver who triggered the reaction.

Let's look at what might happen. Let's say a girl has been raised by a mother who was critical and highly judgmental of other women's physical appearances, always making negative comments about their weight or attire. Later in life, the woman who has been mothered in this way becomes uncomfortable whenever her partner looks at her a bit too long. If the partner makes any comment at all about her appearance, whether positive or negative, she becomes defensive and retreats. She begins to react as if she is dealing with a person who will be judgmental and disapprove of her. The partner is not being seen for who he is, how he really behaves, or what he is saying to her. Instead, he is seen behind a coating of unfinished business that has been cast on top of him from her needed work with her mother.

As another example, suppose a young adult male has a female boss, and he believes that he is always disappointing her. In fact, he fears that he might be fired, even though his job performance is great and he is always rated highly on his performance reviews. His fear is real. This is the foreground. The background is that he had a physically and emotionally abusive mother who berated him when he was between the ages of three and seven and told him she wished he had never been born. He does not remember her beratement until he stops and really looks back.

This type of projection may come from within a person. "You look tired," a friend says to you. You may not actually be tired, but your friend is tired and projects his weariness onto you. These are all examples of the first format of projection: assigning to others what is actually being held within ourselves.

Clients are more likely to use this type of projection when they have not worked on their unfinished business from their past. It becomes fodder when the subconscious is struggling to deal with the present situation. An overlay of sorts is created and projected onto the other person, although the person projecting does not consciously realize they are doing this.

The second format of projection occurs when a person shifts the boundary between themselves and the rest of the world a little too much in their own favor. The person disavows or disowns parts of self or personality they find offensive or aspects of themselves that are not fully within their awareness. They cast the disowned part of self upon someone who displays this behavior outright, and they disapprove of the person who is triggering what is actually internal to them but outside their awareness. It is easier to clearly see and express their reaction to the other person than it is to look within and work on themselves. This is a common pattern. In essence, we can see issues in someone else, but we cannot see the same issues in ourselves.

For instance, a person does not see herself as a gossip, but she leans over to a friend and whispers, "I just cannot stand our new board member. She is such a gossip!" The part of herself that is a gossip is outside of her present awareness.

Through Gestalt, all parts are examined, and once a person sees the fullness of their personality, they can avoid this projective state.

Confluence

Boundaries become diffused when we are in a state of confluence. Parts of self and the wholeness of the self are indistinguishable from those of another person. This is often seen when there is enmeshment in a relationship, but it is especially important to be identified in the coaching relationship. This occurs when the coach has unfinished business, and as they become triggered by another, they no longer see that person as separate from their own self in their thoughts or feelings. The lines become blurry because they conjoin with the other by superimposing their own experience, feelings, and thoughts onto the other person.

It is important for coaches to have done their own work on their life's unfinished business. For instance, if a coach went through a contentious divorce after their mate had an affair but the coach has never addressed it in their personal Gestalt work, they may still carry unfinished business around their anger and resentment. Years later, a client sits before them and begins to speak about their concern that their mate is having an affair and the pain that causes for them.

The coach may become confluent and begin to assume the client will be ending their marriage as they have done. Once confluent, they are no longer hearing the client as a separate person, and confusion may set in. The client leaves the process perhaps confused because they intended to examine their part in their partner's affair and wanted to work on saving their relationship.

This is especially inappropriate in a session when the client begins to express something about themselves and triggers the coach's own unfinished business. It is out of integrity to be in a professional relationship with a client with whom you become confluent. In this case, the coach is no longer in contact with the client and is no longer hearing the unique thoughts and feelings of the client. The coach cannot cleanly assist the client while in this state. Likened to jumping in and flowing down a river with the other person in a state of commiseration, the relationship has stopped being a place of contact from which each person connects in personal authenticity. Healing can no longer occur.

In our programs, we are proactive in that our coaches have done the majority of their personal work on their unfinished business while in training and before becoming certified. While this is not a requirement of most traditional therapy degrees, it is a key requirement for Gestalt institutes everywhere.

Deflection

Deflection is similar to confluence in that no true contact is made between sender and receiver when the receiver is deflecting because a statement made by the sender bounces off the receiver as if they have a shield preventing them from taking it in. The sender feels unheard, and the receiver cheats themselves from hearing what the sender has said.

Often a result of poor self-esteem or a fear of criticism, the receiver unwittingly blocks or denounces any positive feedback or messages as being untrue.

Deflection is a method or maneuver to turn away or take the heat out of direct contact. It shows up in behaviors like laughing off a compliment, not looking the sender in the eye, discounting what the other person has said, coming up with contrary examples, or even mutely shrugging a shoulder.

Retroflection

Retroflection is a state in which the energy turns sharply back against the sender. Clients who present a shut down or depressed affect often require an exploration of whether it is caused by being in the state of retroflection. This occurs when the person has an unsupported ability to express their anger or their personal truth to another to finish the process. The flow of anger turns back on the sender and manifests in a myriad of behaviors.

Retroflection is like a boomerang. Let's say that anger arises for the client but the client is unable to direct that anger at the person for whom it is felt. Their inability may stem from being afraid of the person with whom they are angry or it may even stem from inexperience with expressing anger at all. Like a boomerang, the anger returns to the person experiencing it, both energetically and behaviorally. This may manifest in cutting, overdrinking, overeating, or other self-destructive behaviors. In this state, the person treats himself as he originally wanted to treat another person or object. By redirecting activity inward, he substitutes himself for the intended target. It is as if he is splitting himself in two, one part the "doer" and the other part the "done to."

In its most deepened state, retroflection spirals a person downward to thoughts of self-harm, and it can lead to suicide. When redirected outward to the original target in a safe Gestalt experiment, the release can free the client from this self-destructive state. Gestalt is a perfect medium to assist a person in releasing this pent up anger in a safe way, allowing for clarity to move the energy, thoughts, and emotions in a more productive direction.

The person's self-esteem may lack the strength to fully direct the anger to the intended receiver. When the sender's self-esteem is beginning to rise, we may see them use displacement instead of retroflection. Now, instead of turning the energy into a boomerang and back to self, the person directs it to a target less intimidating than the person who gave rise to the anger in the first place. Usually this target is completely blindsided since they are not the originating source of the anger.

Let's say someone is angry with their boss at work. They feel neither prepared nor able to speak directly to their boss for fear of being demoted or fired. In a retroflected state, they may leave work and risk their life by driving crazily on the freeway. Or they might stop at a fast food restaurant and binge on fast food before dinner. Or they might cut themselves in their cubicle before heading home. If, on the other hand, they displace their anger instead of retroflecting it, they will drive home and yell at their spouse or kick their dog.

My own father often drank too much in the evenings. He held a very high position in our community and was quite successful in his work life. When I was a young adult, he would invite me over for dinner. He loved to cook and made terrific meals. However, by the time the food was set on the table, he had been drinking scotch for a couple of hours. He became a belligerent person, verbally abusive and cynical about life.

By my early twenties, I decided to speak up about how I felt about his excessive drinking whenever I came over for dinner. Time and time again, I rehearsed what I was going to say as I was driving over, but when I got to his home, I would not want to cause a scene or a fight, so I would hold back and not tell him how I felt. I usually overate, and after leaving, I felt down on myself and out of sorts.

I finally worked on it in my Gestalt work. I planned to stop retroflecting on myself and instead, I spoke with him at his office one morning about his drinking. I told him I understood he had the full right to drink in his own home and I was not telling him he could not drink. However, I was choosing in the future to only meet him for breakfast or lunch in a restaurant. I would not be coming over to his house for dinner in the future. By taking my own power without telling him he had to change his lifestyle, I had found a solution. I could live with myself and let go of his decisions about his life and relationships.

Resistance as a Gestaltist Views It

These are a few of the most commonly seen defenses employed by all of us at one time or another. Rather than seeing these as bad, wrong, or something to be diagnosed, Gestaltists recognize that as a person becomes more aware of who they are and how they came to be who they are, these defenses used as resistance become less frequently employed. The peace the client achieves in knowing their true self and having clarity around all unfinished business stops the need to defend.

The job of the coach is to identify and recognize the different defenses a client is employing. The piece of work is often designed with the defense in mind. Resistances are red flags for the coach to identify when the work holds a background versus something that is totally in the present for the client.

As I sit with a client, I may hear a statement that is counter to other facts I know about them. This may be an introjection that we need to explore. In the 1980s, I sat with Dan as he spoke of his loneliness. He worked for the telephone company, and back then, things were done differently than today. Daily, Dan was scaling seventy-foot poles with a belt around his body and cleats on his shoes.

While sharing about something unrelated to his work, Dan said, "I'm very clumsy. I've always been a clumsy guy. It's why I'm single. Who would ever want to be with a clumsy man?"

Really? I thought. *And you're working seventy feet off the ground with electricity? How can this be true?* I felt that he had introjected this, and I wanted to find out when and how.

After establishing his trust in me, I asked him to close his eyes and allow me to state back to him what he had told me. I instructed him to allow himself to listen and pay attention to where he felt the statements in his body, allowing himself to explore his past and find when he first heard the statements. "You are clumsy, you are so clumsy, you are just a clumsy guy," I repeated a few times to Dan.

Dan's eyes opened with tears in them as he shared with me a memory from when he was about six years old. He was at the family dinner table, and his parents had been quarreling over something. Dan reached for his milk glass and accidentally tipped the glass over on the table. He remembered it flowing quickly toward his father's end of the table and onto his dad's lap. His dad stood up with his pants soiled and screamed at Dan, "You are always a clumsy brat! You are always so stupid and clumsy!" His father stormed from the dining room, his mother started crying, and his older brother laughed at him.

For six-year-old Dan, it felt like some truth about himself that he did not know until that moment. And because it had come from his father, who he thought knew everything, it must be true. Further, not being old enough to have a fully formed understanding of who he really was, he swallowed it whole and had believed it ever since.

As Dan recounted the memory, I began to work with reframing his reality by asking him to see that he climbed telephone poles in a highly dangerous job—something that demanded coordination. I also knew he'd rode horses since he was a kid as a "roper," which is also an event that takes talent and coordination. We gently unpacked the truth of who he was and how differently it defined him from his lifelong belief of himself.

He told me he lost a girlfriend he cared about because she wanted to take dance lessons together or do some surfing and he was convinced he was too clumsy. He had always thought golf looked like fun but felt he knew he was too clumsy for it. And he had even limited his job hunting prospects because he was sure he was stupid and clumsy.

After this reexamination, Dan was able to speak to his dad in an empty chair and hand it all back to him, where it truly belonged. This was freeing Dan to form and accept a new self-concept that better served him in his life. He not simply talked about the incident, but spoke to his dad and told him how he felt as a child when the incident happened and how unfair and wrong his dad was to not handle the milk spilling as an accident. He told his dad that the way he handled the situation had made it a part of Dan's identity. Dan could acknowledge that he was hurt and angry that his dad didn't understand that.

The dialogue he held with his dad in the empty chair put the truth back into perspective. It was a mistake his father had made, and the milk spillage was an accident, not a federal crime. This also allowed Dan to begin to see his father as a human being who made mistakes and to move to a more authentic relationship with him. Dan was able to feel self-compassion for his younger self and recognize that his inner child had needed the release provided by the empty chair exercise.

When an unfinished background is there, the person is often said to be overreacting in some situation they are dealing with in their present life. This cues the coach to ask questions to uncover the incident in the past. If a person is having difficulty in their present life, but there is no unfinished business, they are not in a state of being triggered and are often expressing around it in a responsive and calm state.

12

From the Mind to the Body

The mind is the great trickster. It is often rewinding, replaying, and creating thoughts at a rapid speed. And this pattern of rampant thoughts is rarely kept in the present moment. Instead, it darts between past and future, creating justifications, denials, rationalizations, plans, and fantasies that keep the thinker away from what is actually in the present. This is a seductive dance that robs the person of living their life. It also creates a reality of being all mind, divorced from the input and knowledge the body provides.

The Gestaltist assists clients in increasing their awareness of their body somatics or energies. Attention is also placed on the emotional field related to the present rather than the reactionary quality of the mind's dance. Asking how they are feeling *now* and bringing awareness to the environment they are presently in, the beings they are relating with, and their experience of life in the moment can assist a person to be in the body rather than being a walking head in a detached state.

Neither anxiety nor depression are based on the present moment. With anxiety, the focus is often on the future; with depression, it is often on the past. In either case, the person is worrying and working themselves up about something other than the now. Both are unproductive and, in fact, can damage a person's physical health.

My second child, Molly, was born with a rare disease. No one knew how she became afflicted with it, and she was one of only three in the world with it. Her disease resulted in surgeries for her, the first when she was only thirty-six hours old. Over the span of twenty-four years, she had twenty-eight surgeries, including two that were transplants. We were in the emergency room and she was an inpatient in hospitals for several days or weeks several times a year. This continued for her entire life.

In addition to that, she was one of the rare people in the world allergic (anaphylactic) to Versed, which is a relaxant drug given to people before surgery so they don't remember going from pre-op into the actual operating room. In Molly's case, she went in stone cold awake to greet the surgeon and the team that would administer anesthesia and perform surgery.

As a mom facing a life of repeated surgeries and painful procedures for my child, I knew I needed to find a strategy that would work for her, one that would help her avoid anxiety or depression by staying in the present moment. I did not want her disease to be the center of her whole identity. I knew she was so much more than that. I decided to be proactive in teaching her present moment skills to the extreme. These she employed all twenty-four years of her life, right up until her last breath.

As many children do, there were a few words she had trouble pronouncing. At three she would know she had surgery coming up and would start to tell me, "Mommy, I don't want to go to the *hopsital*."

I would softly reply, "Molly, I agree, and are we at the hospital right now?"

"No."

"Where are we now?"

"In the barn with Jojo." (Jojo was her pony.)

"That's right. So let's be here with Jojo now, and we will pay attention to the hospital when we are there. Deal?"

She would laugh and say, "Yep!"

This went on in many forms for all of her surgeries. On the way to the hospital I'd play songs in the car we could sing to. "Well, right now we're singing songs, right?" I would say to remind her.

"Yep!"

She wore headphones, with me in a sterile gown by her side, until the anesthesiologist had her completely under. Then I would retreat, fall apart for a few minutes, and wait.

None of this was an attempt at distraction, an attempt to divert attention and thought. That was not the point. The point was that whatever short time she was going to have on the planet, it was important to be fully present in each moment. And with surgeries, the actual pain might last two days post-op—but not the twenty-three days prior to the surgery.

When she came out of the operating room and the pain drugs were wearing off, she would tell me, "Mommy, right now I'm in pain."

"I see that, Molly," I'd reply, "and I'm here with you. We will get through this." And we would work to get her through those painful hours or days.

All her life, Molly employed this way of being like a pro. Through all of her surgeries and at each age, she listened to the doctors, asked questions about procedures, spoke her truth to the medical team, and took all of it as it came. And every moment she was not in the hospital, she was living life to the fullest!

As soon as she was released, we stopped focusing on the hospital stay and her illness. If she told me how much she didn't like it, I would listen to her because that was her real feeling in the moment. But if she looked forward in worry or anxiety, which was extremely rare, it would only be a moment before she decided not to trade a present good moment with useless time spent worrying about what the future might hold.

From her childhood on, she knew what death was, having lost many young friends she knew from the hospital along the way. She was never a person to waste a moment of concern about the "maybe someday" part of her destiny.

Molly's case is an unusual and even extreme example of what is possible, and I'm blessed to have been her mother. She has been my greatest teacher.

As a mom, I did not waste precious life force with Molly by being in a state of worry. We took each step as it came.

Many of those steps were extremely difficult and painful for both of us. But at the end of her life, we had no regrets about how we handled our time together and how we dealt with her disease. We cherished each present moment we had and were careful not to create unfinished business along the way.

In the process of working with clients, I often find it is a more natural state for them to speak or process from their mind. That is often a circular experience full of unproductive processes, such as the query "Why?" That question leads to a state of confusion as a person searches for a one-pronged answer to a multipronged situation that takes them in a futile circle. Though highly unsatisfying, it is in the nature and temperament of the majority of people to search for a simple answer to something far more complex in an attempt to explain why.

As a Gestaltist, my desire is to quest after better trails by asking "How?" That query leads us to when and where the pain began, and the story the client has inside will be laid out more clearly.

Implosion, Body Language, and the Chakra System

Through living life and interacting with others, situations will arise that resemble or are similar to a person's trauma or unresolved experiences in their background. These often cause the person to have a reaction—or even an overreaction—instead of a response. The reactive state is a clue that there is something in the client's background that is unfinished. The mind has creatively found ways to repress the memory or distract the person from looking too closely at the upsetting occurrence in their past. This method of keeping unfinished business seemingly locked away and out of awareness is called implosion. The imploded state is one of contraction, frozenness, and compression of self.

These imploded experiences often reveal themselves to the client during the process of working with the Gestaltist. The client's usual strategy of retaining their unfinished business is disrupted, causing stress and anxiety. We call this perturbation. In physics, perturbation is a deviation from a normal or regular state caused by an outside influence. In Gestalt work, the Gestaltist is the outside influence causing the state of perturbation in the client. The client might state that they feel nauseous, have a headache, or are experiencing other body symptoms.

As the coach asks questions and creates a space of safety and listening that is deeper than usually experienced by the client, the client's "stuff" begins to emerge or rise up in their body. Their usual strategy of retaining their unfinished business presses downward in energy from their mind. This causes implosion.

As the piece of work in a Gestalt session opens up and unfolds to the background, the implosion often results in an explosion of awareness and emotions in the client that lead to finishing a piece of the unfinished business in their life and psyche. This creates for the client the healthier state of responding to triggers as separate experiences and not reacting to them from an unaware state.

In the Gestalt Coaching Method, we work with implosion a bit differently from other Gestalt work because I have folded in my studies of somatics and other modalities. In the early years of my psychotherapy studies, I became interested in the study of body language. This is the process of communicating nonverbally through conscious or unconscious gestures and movements. Body language is our communication without or in conjunction with words. It is anything someone does nonverbally to which someone else assigns meaning. For instance, a person in session may place their hand over their heart as they say, "I am heartbroken." The nonverbal communication supports or validates the verbal communication. Not all of the nonverbal signals a person sends are intentional, and they are often either not picked up on by others or worse, misinterpreted.

About the same time I became interested in body language, I was also beginning my studies of the energy fields in the human body. Although this had been a part of Eastern medicine for centuries, it was rather new thought in psychotherapy in the 1980s, and I was curious to explore energy fields for myself.

One day I had an epiphany. Could body language and energy fields be related somehow? And could words be a part of it too? I had never heard or read of such a connection, but I was witnessing it daily with my clients. Could a person be expressing their subconscious body language in conjunction with words, and could it also tie in to the chakra energy fields in the body? I was pretty sure that the answer was yes.

As I observed my clients over the next year, I noticed that it was undeniable how these things intertwined. And I found it very helpful in designing creative Gestalt experiments.

If a person was feeling unsafe or without basic necessities, they would often express verbally while moving their feet, shifting in their seat, and even sometimes stating that their tailbone was in pain. The body language correlated to the first chakra, known as the root chakra, which represents foundation, security, safety, and basic needs being met or unmet.

If a client was expressing feeling stuck, unproductive, or sexually repressed, their hands would often be on their lower abdomen or their lower back. They sometimes spoke of pain, dysfunction, constipation, or bowel issues. This tied in to the second or sacral chakra, which relates to production, birthing, sexual energy, and pouring forth.

Clients would show up in fear or anxiety about a decision they wanted to make, touching their solar plexus as they expressed their feelings of uncertainty. As the work progressed and they found their way through to a feeling of personal power and clarity, they would vocalize determination to go in a certain direction. It was not uncommon for them to place their hand on their hips or pat their midriff confidently. This correlated to the third or solar plexus chakra, which is the center of fear, will, and determination.

A heartbroken client would often wring their hands or place a hand over their heart as they leaked tears and spoke of grief or a broken love relationship. This correlated to the fourth or heart chakra, the center of love, empathy, and compassion, embodying the things that their words and body were so clearly signaling.

When I would suggest to a client that they needed to tell someone in their life something that was difficult to say, they sometimes placed their hand over their throat or mouth in

The Chakras

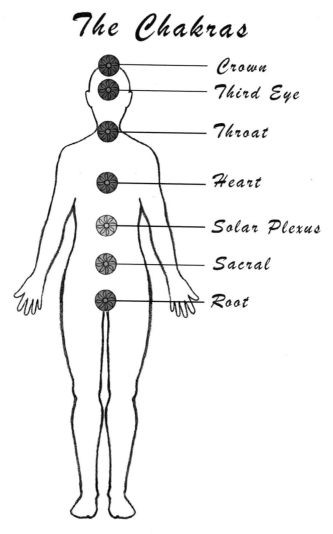

- Crown
- Third Eye
- Throat
- Heart
- Solar Plexus
- Sacral
- Root

hesitation and said, "I can't tell him that!" Again, their body language backed up their thoughts, and the motion to the fifth or throat chakra was fitting because that chakra governs what is expressed or unexpressed.

When a person had a complex or overwhelming issue that they did not want to explore, they would often take their hand to their brow and rub back and forth as they said, "Oh, I just don't know. I just don't know." They were rubbing the area of the sixth or brow chakra, the seat of intuition or inexplicable knowingness.

When in total crisis, clients would place their hands on top of their head and say, "Oh, my God." This was the perfect gesture and statement for the seventh or crown chakra, which resides on top of the skull and relates to connection with Source.

I loved playing with this understanding in Gestalt work because it gave me so many clues by simply observing my clients as they expressed themselves. And I found I could count on it adding to a better understanding of the total person. Not only words, but subconscious body language, action, body sensations, and energy fields all came forth together to express a fuller picture.

Because I was interested in implosion, I wanted to understand how it formed and what the energy of implosion was telling me about my client. Could there be a further clue? A second epiphany hit me hard. Not only was body language keyed to what a person was verbally saying, but the chakra fields were involved in the client's sensations. And the sensations were coordinated and located at the implosion spots that my clients were expressing as pain or discomfort in their physical body.

This information opened up new clues and productive ways of working with my clients in a more effective and efficient manner. Combining the power of Gestalt with all of these other modalities and techniques helped guide the formation of both the Gestalt Coaching Method and the Equine Gestalt Coaching Method.

By asking questions that seemed to be out of left field but were actually based on all of the clues the client's body and mind were putting forth, I began to notice that I could creatively set up experiments, and they were right on the money for the client. For instance, if a client said that he had developed a severe headache on the drive over and might need to cancel the session, I told him to have a seat and asked exactly where the headache was affecting him. If he placed his hand over his brow and said, "All across the front of my forehead," I knew that he was referring to the brow chakra, which related to knowingness and intuition.

"Is there anything you feel you *know* but really don't want to see or know is true?" I would ask, seemingly out of left field.

The client would look up, dumbfounded. "How did you know? I was coming here to see you today because I'm afraid that my wife might be having an affair." His intuition was screaming at him, but every brain cell was full of strategies to protect him from looking at what he was intuiting. The resulting implosion was pain, and once we began a piece of work, the headache lifted right away.

Experiences like this with clients were common. And there is a reason for that. When a client is in a sacred and safe space with the desire to heal their stuff or unfinished business, things begin to bubble up through, within, and across the body somatics. Eventually, this energy becomes lodged or paused in a specific space.

Often, discomfort or physical symptoms emerge as the client's body is communicating to them that implosion is present. But how does the energy of the unfinished business become stopped at that point?

Strategy

My experienced answer to that question is what I call *strategy*. After a traumatic event or a time when life moves forward without allowing a person to finish or complete what they need to do or say, the mind takes over. In a desire to protect oneself, the subconscious mind knits complex patterns to assist in avoiding memories of the situation. These patterns may present in numerous forms: minimizing, creating limiting beliefs, changing of the subject, and a whole host of behaviors to circumvent the person from "going there"—from reclaiming those memories. It is painful to go there since it is unfinished business and causes frustration.

The client's strategy, which is completely outside of their awareness, works to an extent to keep them comfortable. But there is one big problem: Situations arise that have just enough of the same plasma or similarity to actually trigger the client to be in a state of reaction instead of having a detached response.

This reactive state can destroy marriages, parenting, work relationships—you name it. Like a hidden minefield, the situations trigger the client, and they don't understand why something bothers them so much. But it does. Such an event is sometimes what sends them to seek help to understand themselves better.

To the coach, the client's strategy may appear as changing the subject, moving around and walking off, deflection through joking around, becoming upset, drinking, smoking pot, or other forms of avoidance.

When a well-trained Gestalt coach recognizes avoidance of a subject as the client strategy, the gateway to the work can begin. The client's work of identifying the strategy and owning it while discovering the root cause becomes the journey. The goal? To finish the unfinished business, but even more importantly, to experience self-compassion. In the end, there is no place for shame around these strategic behaviors. Instead, what is needed is a sense of gratitude for its formation as a protective mechanism until the time and place comes for it to be safely explored. Within this context, these strategic behaviors can even be blessed.

Exploring the body symptomology as the discussion is deepening between client and coach is a great place to begin. Assisting the progression from being a walking head asking "Why?" to being a fully aware, present in the here and now, and careful listener to their body's messages is all part of the package.

For example, a client may be talking about how her dad is someone she is not close to and how she chooses to avoid him. "He never abused me," she states, but while talking and settling in to the safe place around her, she adds, "I'm feeling nauseous. Maybe it's something I ate."

I reply, "Stay with the feeling," and we continue our journey, talking about her father.

She continues to become uncomfortable and says she is really feeling sick to her stomach.

I pull a wastebasket over. "It's okay. It's your body sending you a signal that you are needing to release something that's troubling you. Let it come." We continue probing a bit, and I ask her to give her stomach or her nausea a voice. "If your stomach had a message, what would it be?"

She blurts out, "I'm sick of it!"

I encourage her to say it again. She does.

"Look inside. What is *it*?" I ask. Moving the wastebasket closer and following her energy, I ask, "What is the *it* that is making you sick?"

Subconsciously, she places her hand over her stomach—her third chakra, the place of fear, but also the place of will and determination. "The *it* is my father intimidating me!"

"Good. Say more," I reply while pulling a pillow closer to us.

From this state, I encourage her to speak to him on that pillow. "See him sitting there and tell him your truth. Tell him from this place of nausea. Tell him!"

She begins. "You intimidated me. You were a bully! I was frightened of you. I was always walking on eggshells. I can remember you hollering at Mom and threatening her. Our house was peaceful until you came home after work and had your highball. I can still hear the ice hitting the glass, knowing it would change you. So I hid in my room."

With a bit of encouragement and some reframing, she continues to say what she could not say back then. She says what would not have been tolerated or safe to express when her inner self really needed to say it.

Words become hard to find. Her strategy has stepped aside. I keep her in this state, knowing it is a rare window. "Make a sound at your father. Find the sound in your body that has been kept inside all these years."

She starts a growl, timidly at first. Again seizing the opening, I encourage her to give it voice with strength and volume. She screams and howls from her solar plexus—no words, just letting her body release the pent up sound, exhausting herself.

I allow her to rest but not totally recover and return to her head, where old strategies may reappear.

"What do you still need to say to your father?"

She gives herself permission to release her truth, and she speaks her bottom-line truth to him, a truth she has harbored for thirty years. Finally, she takes a deep breath.

"How does your stomach feel?" I ask.

She is surprised as she checks in and is better than fine. She says she feels free and clear.

Gently, we begin to process what she has just gone through. I ask her to journal and to move into self-compassion as she reflects on the experience. Because she has released, let go, and finished up what she had to say, do, and feel, there has been a shift. I assure her that she will feel a shift when she speaks to her father the next time. In fact, the relationship will shift without her ever needing to say any of this to him, personally or in real time.

I trust the process and know that if she does decide to speak to him about her feelings, it will now be from a finished and clear place of her truth, not from a jumbled, fear-driven, incohesive, reactive place. And she will listen to her body for further clues.

Some clients struggle with listening to their body. It is a foreign concept for many. Bringing an increasing awareness of the treasure trove of information available to them at all times from their body is a new discovery. It is the job of the practitioner to make this journey a smooth one by introducing the topic of what the client's body is telling them and then adding to the client's awareness through guidance, breathing, and identifying the information. The coach strengthens and supports the client's comments about what is happening and encourages them to translate the information coming through somatically.

Aspects of Consciousness

Thousands of scholars over the centuries have attempted to quantify and define what consciousness is. There is no agreement on definition or explanation of why or how it occurs. Although there is a strong debate between science and philosophy about it, many of us in the coaching field have moved on to grasp some current understandings to work with people.

In the field of psychology, the mind, or psyche, is referred to as having different parts: the conscious mind and the unconscious (or subconscious) mind. Freud used the terms *subconscious* and *unconscious* interchangeably in his writing and lectures. He saw them as the repressed parts of the mind that held memories and feelings that were making the subject ill. These repressed parts of the mind could be revealed in slips of the tongue and in dreams.

As the world of psychology divided toward and away from Freud's concepts, the Humanistic Movement, of which Gestalt is a part, felt strongly that the levels of consciousness were, in fact, quite different. And it did not see the unconscious and subconscious as equivalent.

The conscious mind is in operation when we are in the here and now, the present moment. The thoughts and feelings that we are aware of are in the now, and we can put words to or constructs around them. This is our ego.

The subconscious refers to the part that exists outside of our present awareness in the moment. It stores memories, feelings, and thoughts. The information contained in the subconscious mind is not actively in our awareness, but it still influences us. And most importantly, it is available to us in recall. With focus and concentration, these parts can be awakened and shifted into the forefront of the conscious mind.

The unconscious is the part of the mind we do not have access to and that is not available for recall. It is acting as more of an operating system for the brain. This may be thought of as the warehouse of our thought processes, affects, and memory. The unconscious is not a place where we can be introspective. Our primal and primitive thought, our earliest preverbal understanding, and possibly epigenetic thought patterns lie here. This is the id.

Hypnotherapy is believed to tap in to the subconscious part of the mind in its deepest sections or recesses. It is done for the purpose of tapping in to that which is not consciously processed. Hypnotherapy is useful for retrieving memories and for assisting a person in changing patterns and behavior.

The work in Gestalt often facilitates accessing what is held in the subconscious as well. The client sometimes moves into an altered state of consciousness, which allows them to safely retrieve parts of their memories that are pushed down in their unfinished business. As the client becomes more mindful and aware of the present moment, the coach artfully creates the experiment or piece of work, allowing the client to move into a retrieval state. In the process, the mind frees up the subconscious to complete the work emotionally and cognitively.

These memories are held in the subconscious (sometimes referred to as the *preconscious*) mind, but are accessible. And when the piece of work is completed and a gestalt is achieved, there is a sense of peace and freedom because the client no longer has to expend the energy to keep what has been held in the subconscious in place there.

As we work in mindfulness, encouraging awareness as the key to healing, the client begins to welcome the falling into place of each piece of their personal puzzle. Personally, I agree with Dr. Deepak Chopra's early work, *Perfect Health*, in which he describes how each cell has a brain inside of it. The brain in each cell holds on to memories. As cells die off and new cells come on to replace them, the memories of trauma and unfinished business are replicated and passed on to the new generation of cells. Thus, the body holds the trauma until it is cleared and let go.

This is why Gestalt is so effective. It reaches beyond the conscious mind, releases the subconscious mind from what is trapped there, and encourages the full body and every cell to release pain. It unlocks the brain inside every cell of the body and replaces it with peace, which is then replicated in new cells. We become healthy in body, mind, spirit, and emotions as the process unfolds.

In my work, I experience opportunities to heal people who have kept pain or limiting beliefs in their cells and even DNA across generations. While I was leading a retreat in Montana one summer, a young woman in her thirties expressed how bound she felt by the six generations of ranch women who were her heritage. She had utmost respect for all of them and felt quite blessed to be a born and bred rancher alongside her husband. But the world had changed so much, and she was feeling suppressed somehow. This feeling of suppression, she explained, was not coming from anything the women who preceded her had said directly. Rather, it was an overall feeling she said she carried in her genes.

I asked five women from the group to stand up and then stand in a line as if waiting in a teller line at the bank. Because of the setting, it happened that two of the five women were also wives of ranchers and had been raised in multigenerational ranch families.

My client, Jo, faced the first woman, and I told her to imagine this was her mother. I asked her to notice the line of women behind her and explained that these were the women of each generation behind her mom—her grandmother, great-grandmother, and so on. I then coached her to speak her truth to her mom. What was it Jo most needed her mom to understand about being a woman rancher today?

She thought long and hard, then she raised her eyes to the woman standing in for her mom. "Mom, I am truly grateful to you, as your daughter. I've learned to respect you and myself. Mom, it's hard for me to say to you, but I'm not pulled or called to have children of my own." Jo took a deep breath as tears filled her eyes. "Mom, I have a different vision of living on the ranch. I love driving the big ten-ton baler and the tractors. I love being my husband's full partner and love that we both work to take care of the ranch and ourselves. Mom, I know this is quite different from how you lived, and I hope you can respect my choices."

I had asked the people in the lineup to remain present but silent, speaking from their eyes only. I handed Jo a box of Kleenex to act as a prop. "Jo," I said, "this represents your handing some of the traditions that don't fit you today back to your mom."

She handed the woman representing her mom the box and said, "Mom, here are the traditions I return to you, and I lovingly keep the others you have taught me."

I then asked Jo to stand with her mom behind her as she spoke to her grandmother. "Grandma, I can remember you always kept a warm home," she said. "You worked so hard to prepare meals for everyone—both family and hands. Your kids were hardworking and respectful, even if sometimes mischievous. I remember you working with your hands and rarely sitting down except to work at a sewing machine. Grandma, my life is so different, and I am grateful you were my grandma. I hope I don't disappoint you when I say I'm not anyone's cook or maid. It is important to me and Bill, my husband, that we share in our life, inside and out. I'm on the tractor just as he is, and we haul the hay to the dealer together. And at home, we cook side by side. And if laundry needs doing, whoever is closest to the machine handles it."

She gently handed her surrogate grandmother the box. "With this, I respectfully hand the traditions and roles that were in your generation back to you as I lovingly accept my own."

We then held similar conversations all the way back through the generations. Jo had a lot of knowledge of her heritage and what each time in history held—World War II, World War I, and all the way back to the first generation who came to America.

Once the box was in the hands of her ancestor who first came to America, I asked each woman playing a part to give the box back to Jo with a one-word blessing honoring her. They gave her love, peace, strength, respect, glory, and joy as they honored the ranch woman today they felt in Jo.

Jo wept sweet tears and was embraced by all who were present. There was a wonderful sharing afterward in the group. Everyone understood at least part of the experience because it related to their own life.

In this kind of exercise, the release that is experienced by the client brings peace into their soul. Great borrowed benefit is also experienced because those standing in the place of the generations and those observing the work are deeply touched and challenged in their own processes to reexamine their own life as well.

Release and Return to the Present Moment

When the work focuses on body somatics, traumas that have been held in the body are released, body and mind can work effectively together instead of being at odds with one another, and the client is returned to the present moment. And it is in the present moment that real awareness happens.

13

Awareness Cycle

Life is all about energy. Gestalt follows energy. Remember when you were in high school and you studied molecules, electrons, protons, and all of that stuff? That "stuff" is what makes up life itself. Those molecules are moving inside our bodies, around our bodies, and everywhere between our bodies and everything else. Just as gravity is invisible yet real and love is invisible yet real, energy is real.

As a Gestaltist, I pay attention to my own energy and that of my client. As energy moves, it creates a pathway for discovery. In Gestalt, we observe the "awareness energy" in a cycle. Many authors and trainers have attempted to explain how the cycle flows and have developed charts and models to explain it.

The basic cycle is usually depicted as an arched line. The important takeaway is that this cycle is occurring all of the time. In fact, several cycles can be at play at one time. An awareness energy cycle can be interrupted or it can flow smoothly.

The most basic description is often taught with this example: You are sitting on a sofa, maybe reading a book. This is the *withdrawal* stage. Your mouth is dry and your throat tightens slightly when you swallow. This is the *sensations* stage. Your mind begins to form the awareness that you are thirsty. This is the *awareness* stage. You put down your book, stand up, and walk into the kitchen to get a glass of water. This is the *mobilization of energy* stage. You lift the glass to your lips, begin to drink the water, and swallow. This is the *action* stage. Your throat is now soft, your mouth is wet, and you are no longer thirsty. This is the *contact* stage. You might go back to the sofa or move to do something else, since your thirst is quenched. Once again, you are in *withdrawal*.

Okay, so that is a very basic look at the awareness arch, explaining in everyday terms how this awareness cycle operates.

Let's look at another example. A coach has a group session with eight clients. During the first hour of group, she works with one of the clients. In the second hour, she notices that there is time to work with another person in the group. The coach makes the invitation and waits for one of the clients to claim the space. She notices that some group members are squirming and adjusting their positions, looking left and right. Finally, one person, Alyssa, begins to move forward and says, "I can feel a headache coming on." She laughs and adds, "So I'd like to work."

What just happened? Alyssa was sitting in a neutral space observing the last piece of work and sharing her emotions with the group. As the coach stated that there was time for another piece of work, the energy shifted from a more neutral space, and Alyssa noticed her headache forming (sensation).

Shortly thereafter, she thought to herself (awareness) that this was her opportunity to work, and she volunteered to come forward (mobilization).

Now, getting up from her pillow, she moves to the pillow that is open before the coach (action). After sitting down, she begins to breathe deeply and come into contact with the waiting coach (contact). There is a moment of grounding, and this arch is complete (withdrawal).

Let's break it down further and see just what is happening in these two examples. In both cases, the person starts in a state of withdrawal. A perceived body experience, such as discomfort or pain, then arises to the level of sensation. As the body feels the sensation, the mind moves into realization. There is a need to be met. The body interprets what it will need to do to get that need met. This starts a reaction that mobilizes energy, and the person takes an action toward solving the issue at hand.

In the case of Alyssa, when she heard the invitation, she began to experience a headache. Her "stuff" started urging her to take a look at it, while her mind was trying its best to stop it from happening. She began to move and take her place, which mobilized energy and began to meet the need as she took the action to sit in the hot seat. As she came in contact with her coach, the need was being met through contact. And after it was met, she could move back into her former state of withdrawal.

Using the language of energy in my work, I think of and refer to the steps or stations shown on the awareness cycle a bit differently when working with a client. On the energy cycle, the first element is commonly referred to as a state of *withdrawal*. But using the labels of energy, the client may be in a *steady state,* or *equilibrium.* This can also be a state in which opposing forces or influences are in balance. This neutral state, or state of physical balance, is their present normal or familiar state, even if it is not healthy.

As the session begins and a safe and sacred place is before them, the client begins to experience a sensation in their body, which we observe as somatics, the body's energy fields or the tangible organic sensations. The body often identifies and speaks the truth before the mind gives forth thought.

The client is asked to pay attention to their somatics and sit with their sensations—such as a headache, stiff neck, scratchy throat, or the need to move their feet back and forth. They reach a place of awareness in doing so as their mind translates the body somatics to a mental understanding or an interpretation that defines the present need.

To meet the need, the body begins to move, and this mobilizes the energy field toward action, which in a Gestalt session is where the experiment is formed to explore both the somatics and the awareness of the need. The client's energy is mobilized as they begin to tell their story.

As this experiment or the piece of work unfolds, ideally there is a completed Gestalt. A sense of completion is high in the energy field. And this results in the client finding a new equilibrium.

After working with well over a thousand clients, my experience leads me to define and deepen the understanding of how the work overlays onto this energy cycle arch. Let's look now from the coach's perspective.

As our imaginary client, Alyssa, sits with the other seven members of the group, she is personally in equilibrium, but observing or even being a part of the last person's piece of work may have stirred things up from her subconscious. When the coach speaks, Alyssa hears the invitation for another piece of work to be done that evening. More than Alyssa's conscious decision-making process, Alyssa's body quickly reacts and creates a headache across her brow.

This headache is a result of implosion. Her body somatics are stirred up by her unfinished business or "stuff" coming up for examination before her mind moves into awareness and translates the meaning. The mind brings forth what I call a *familiar strategy* instead.

This strategy arises to quiet the urge to explore the unfinished business. It is a familiar pattern formed to protect Alyssa from the pain involved in a memory. This happens very quickly, outside of her awareness, and it has been rehearsed many times in her life. Whenever she attempts to think about or express around a painful trauma or a piece of unfinished business, the pattern arises.

As the strategy clamps down and the somatics rise, a tremendous pressure is created between the two. This creates a state of perturbation or anxiety. As described earlier, perturbation is a process during which energy moves from its regular path or normal state because of an outside influence.

Let's take a look at perturbation outside the realm of individual somatics. An easy example of perturbation found in everyday life is what happens when a pot of water is placed on a stove to boil. Before reaching boiling, the pot sometimes begins to shake, rattle, and dance on the stove instead of moving smoothly into a boil.

Similar to how the pot does the dance on the stove, Alyssa's anxiety is trapped between two opposing forces—one stating there is something held in the body that needs exploration and the other protecting her from looking at it.

Physical pain is often the result.

The coach assists Alyssa in unpacking the awareness of what her body is saying by bringing her attention to the fullness and location of the pain and even by checking to see if the pain itself has something to say.

With any client, as the story unfolds, it often begins with the foreground. This is what they are aware of and logically is a place for them to begin. Further unpacking yields the background—the unfinished business. And as it emerges, what the body is aware of presents itself, even when the mind's strategy is trying to suppress it.

Once the background is discovered, the coach can set up and offer the experiment(s) best suited to explore the unfinished state. This may include a variety of work pieces designed to address the client's needs, and they are graded to meet the client where she is. For example, the coach may introduce an empty chair conversation or a creative reenactment piece. And as the client steps into the piece of work more fully and says or does what is needed to begin closure to the unfinished business, the wholeness of the actual gestalt is achieved. Completion is experienced, and a sense of peace comes over the body.

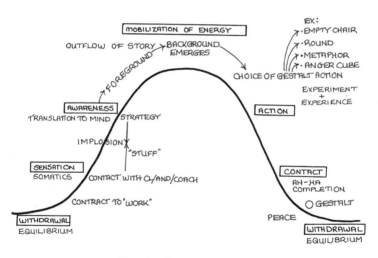

Note: See charts at back of book.

As the body leads the way and awareness is gained, the client's ability to have responses instead of reactions when similar situations occur becomes solid.

For the coach, when the background emerges from the story the client is expressing, there is a moment when the coach decides the "grading" appropriate for the client. The word *grading* is not used here as in the grading of an exam but more like the grading of steepness on a highway. For example, a sign that says the road ahead is at an 8 percent grade alerts the driver to its steepness and the challenges associated with that. While the coach is always looking for creative and useful ways to set up the experience for the client, they must take grading into account.

The design and selection of the piece of work needs to be challenging for the client but not overwhelming. If a client has participated in group process or has had a series of sessions, I might select a piece that would be almost impossible for someone who is in their first experience of this type of work. For a beginning client, completing sentences of truth out loud may be a big enough step, while later, they may speak their truth to someone in an empty chair. Later on, they may release anger with a racket on the cube or experience a recreated and recast scene.

Every client has a different capacity, and it is the responsibility of the coach to correctly gauge what is appropriate grading. The grading allows the client to work in complete safety, and trust is built between the coach and their client. The work layers upon itself, and the grading becomes higher.

The coach's desire is to fully challenge the client to ensure that the background is fully flushed out while not choosing a grading that would overwhelm the client and stop the process. The coach selects and designs the experiment that will be most helpful. This may be the empty chair, a Round, a polarity pole, a metaphor, anger release, primal scream, or another of the many other creative approaches designed to assist the client in moving to the moment of working through the unfinished business. This experiential process of the experiment is fluid and can be changed and redesigned artfully as the piece of work unfolds. The finishing of the business brings corrective closure to it, thereby releasing the body memory from holding onto it and creating pain, either physically or emotionally.

The coach is also working with the energy cycle in terms of observing where breaks may interrupt the cycle. Focusing on the interrupted energy can lead to discoveries of defenses, breaks in contact, and increasing body awareness. Bridging the blockages becomes the framework for the piece of work and stimulates the client's inner liveliness and self-awareness.

The diagrams that follow walk a client named Jim through several examples of possible interruptions in the cycle. As the coach takes this more sophisticated look at the client's behavior, another lens is placed on their discovery process.

1. Complete Cycle

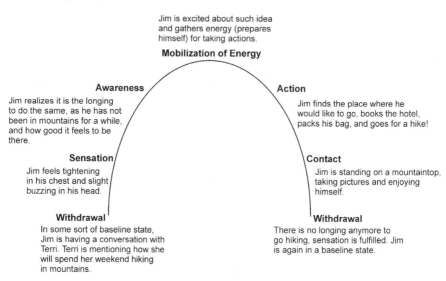

Jim is excited about such idea and gathers energy (prepares himself) for taking actions.

Mobilization of Energy

Awareness

Jim realizes it is the longing to do the same, as he has not been in mountains for a while, and how good it feels to be there.

Action

Jim finds the place where he would like to go, books the hotel, packs his bag, and goes for a hike!

Sensation

Jim feels tightening in his chest and slight buzzing in his head.

Contact

Jim is standing on a mountaintop, taking pictures and enjoying himself.

Withdrawal

In some sort of baseline state, Jim is having a conversation with Terri. Terri is mentioning how she will spend her weekend hiking in mountains.

Withdrawal

There is no longing anymore to go hiking, sensation is fulfilled. Jim is again in a baseline state.

2. Interruption between Withdrawal and Sensation

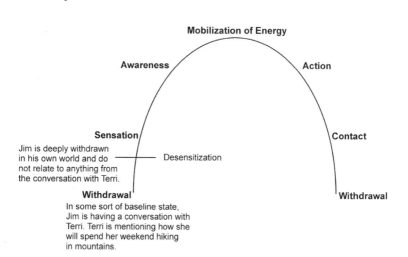

Mobilization of Energy

Awareness

Action

Sensation

Jim is deeply withdrawn in his own world and do not relate to anything from the conversation with Terri.

Desensitization

Contact

Withdrawal

In some sort of baseline state, Jim is having a conversation with Terri. Terri is mentioning how she will spend her weekend hiking in mountains.

Withdrawal

3. Interruption between Sensation and Awareness

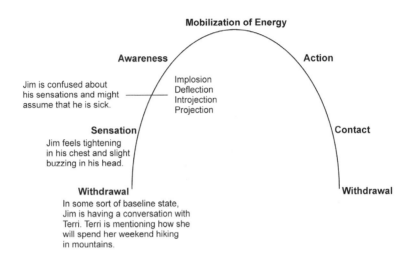

Mobilization of Energy

Awareness   **Action**

Jim is confused about   Implosion
his sensations and might —   Deflection
assume that he is sick.   Introjection
                               Projection

Sensation   **Contact**
Jim feels tightening
in his chest and slight
buzzing in his head.

Withdrawal   **Withdrawal**
In some sort of baseline state,
Jim is having a conversation with
Terri. Terri is mentioning how she
will spend her weekend hiking
in mountains.

4. Interruption between Awareness and Mobilization of Energy

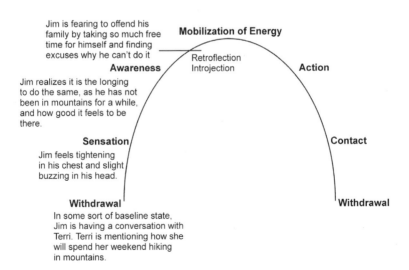

Jim is fearing to offend his
family by taking so much free   **Mobilization of Energy**
time for himself and finding
excuses why he can't do it   Retroflection
Awareness   Introjection   **Action**

Jim realizes it is the longing
to do the same, as he has not
been in mountains for a while,
and how good it feels to be
there.

Sensation   **Contact**
Jim feels tightening
in his chest and slight
buzzing in his head.

Withdrawal   **Withdrawal**
In some sort of baseline state,
Jim is having a conversation with
Terri. Terri is mentioning how she
will spend her weekend hiking
in mountains.

137

5. Interruption between Mobilization of Energy and Action

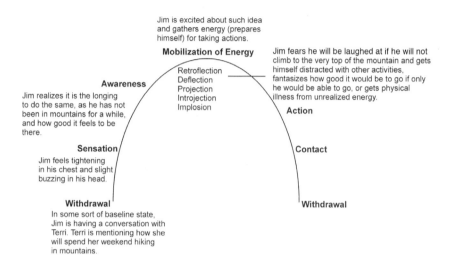

Mobilization of Energy

Jim is excited about such idea and gathers energy (prepares himself) for taking actions.

Awareness

Jim realizes it is the longing to do the same, as he has not been in mountains for a while, and how good it feels to be there.

Retroflection
Deflection
Projection
Introjection
Implosion

Jim fears he will be laughed at if he will not climb to the very top of the mountain and gets himself distracted with other activities, fantasizes how good it would be to go if only he would be able to go, or gets physical illness from unrealized energy.

Action

Sensation

Jim feels tightening in his chest and slight buzzing in his head.

Contact

Withdrawal

In some sort of baseline state, Jim is having a conversation with Terri. Terri is mentioning how she will spend her weekend hiking in mountains.

Withdrawal

6. Interruption between Action and Contact

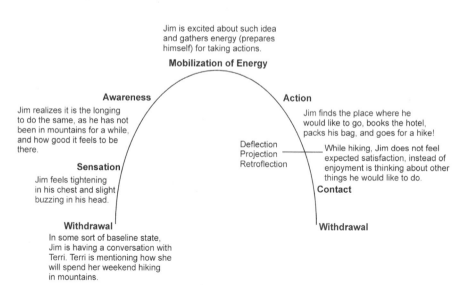

Jim is excited about such idea and gathers energy (prepares himself) for taking actions.

Mobilization of Energy

Awareness

Jim realizes it is the longing to do the same, as he has not been in mountains for a while, and how good it feels to be there.

Action

Jim finds the place where he would like to go, books the hotel, packs his bag, and goes for a hike!

Deflection
Projection
Retroflection

While hiking, Jim does not feel expected satisfaction, instead of enjoyment is thinking about other things he would like to do.

Sensation

Jim feels tightening in his chest and slight buzzing in his head.

Contact

Withdrawal

In some sort of baseline state, Jim is having a conversation with Terri. Terri is mentioning how she will spend her weekend hiking in mountains.

Withdrawal

138

7. Interruption between Contact and Withdrawal

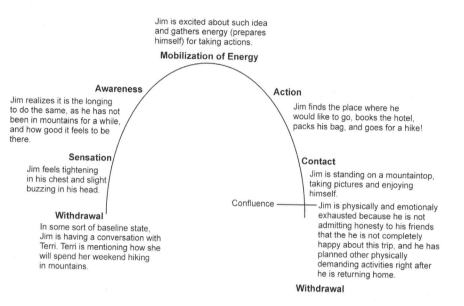

Just as the cycle is a part of every moment in life, so are these breaks in the cycle. This is a complex topic about which volumes can be written, yet for our purposes here, the most important understanding is that these breaks occur. As in most of Gestalt theory, it is less about labeling or making something unhealthy or wrong and far more about expanding our awareness that we all share in the experiences of establishing contact and creating ways (both in and outside of consciousness) to break it.

14

Metaphors

A metaphor relates something to something else in a way that is not literally true. Instead, it draws a comparison between them in a symbolic way. When a horsewoman says, "That horse is the Hercules of the equine world," she is comparing the horse to a mythological character with super-human strength.

In Gestalt, a metaphor is a verbal picture or miniature movie clip that theatrically expresses how a person is feeling or seeing a given situation. This symbolic information is a result of the subconscious creating a pathway to deeper understanding.

Traditionally, Gestalt practitioners use metaphors to liven up the work in both group process and individual sessions. As a part of the experimentation phase, metaphors may be used by the facilitator for all of the members to engage with, peer through, and bounce off of in the self-exploration process.

Most people use metaphors in language, even without awareness that they are doing so. Saying "This sucks" when frustrated, "She's as nervous as a long-tail cat sleeping by a rocking chair" when observing someone with anxiety, "He's a bull in a china shop" about someone's lack of grace or verbal finesse, or "I feel stuffed" after eating exemplify how metaphors show up in our everyday life.

Some people speak, design, and express themselves naturally in terms of metaphors when they are attempting to explain a circumstance occurring in their life. It is their form of self-expression, and they are intuitively connected to their subconscious and less connected to a literal personality. Such a person might say, "I fell through the ice into my lake of depression," rather than saying, "I became depressed."

As a Gestaltist, I feel metaphoric expressions are worthy of further exploration to bring awareness of how the client feels or how they are processing events. In my work, I encourage a process of exploration with a metaphor when one presents itself in a person's speech. And sometimes the client brings a metaphor into the initial phase of their work with me to express and explain what they want to understand.

Consider this example. Sue sits down for her session and begins by telling me she feels as if she were standing on a small, pointy chunk of ice in the ocean and there is no help in sight. Rather than asking her what this means, I ask her to stand up, close her eyes, and imagine standing on the ice chunk. "Position yourself exactly like you are in the metaphor," I say.

She does, and I can see her balancing there.

"What else are you aware of?" I ask.

"I'm stuck," she says, "and no one knows I'm here and in trouble."

"Stay with the feeling and remain aware."

After a few moments, she says, "I'm alone, and no one knows I'm here."

"What else are you aware of?"

"It's getting dark."

"What feelings come up for you as you stand here alone on the ice chunk and it's getting dark?"

"Disbelief. How am I so alone? How is it that no one notices I'm in trouble?"

This process continues for a few minutes, allowing Sue to unfold all that her subconscious has sent her in the form of this picture. I am careful not to add to, edit, or develop her metaphor experience. It is her message from her subconscious, and it is not my job to ask her, for example, if she sees a lighthouse or if the Coast Guard is coming.

Once complete, I ask her to sit down, breathe, and tell me what she just learned about her life. She is surprised that we traveled inside the metaphor. She was expressing being alone on the ice as a picture of her life, but actually experiencing it gave it a deeper meaning. She tells me that she recently made a move across the country, leaving family and old friends in her home state. She changed jobs and bought a home, and she is overwhelmed. She also has yet to meet someone she can call for help if needed. All of her immediate neighbors and coworkers are in couple relationships, and she is feeling lonely.

To her, the metaphor is an ice chunk because a part of her knows it is temporary. She trusts that she will, in fact, make friends and come to know her new community. We then begin to explore more about her life, and more work is initiated.

When a client has not expressed a direct metaphor, I may ask a provocative question and ask them to express their answer in the form of a metaphor. This is also a technique I use with opening a group. For example, I'll ask, "Can you give me a metaphor for how you show up in new groups or situations?" With someone leaving a marriage, I might say, "Can you tell me about your divorce process in terms of a metaphor?" In some cases, I will help them. "Start it off with . . ." or "It is as if . . ." Alternatively, I might give them an example to help them be certain about what I mean by the word *metaphor*. Once they have expressed their metaphor, I focus on the metaphor they create, and the work begins.

The subconscious mind sends gifts of information in many ways, including memories, dreams, and metaphors. Pictorial explanations in settings that feel unreal or strange are played out in the mind as an alternative way to look at a situation. Metaphors can be rich, fertile ground to explore.

I encourage my students to work with metaphors creatively and to explore them with their client. One method is for the coach to align herself next to her client in the imaginary place of the metaphor, imagining along with the client what the metaphor feels like or looks like. The coach is careful not to ask questions or add statements that do not belong to the client, thereby risking prompting the client to go into their conscious mind for the answers. Keeping them in a more altered state, experiencing or "living" the very metaphor that comes forth, allows for fertile answers and information from their subconscious mind.

Sometimes a coach will pose a question in an attempt to find or create a solution. This is a common error. Even questions that are asked to fill out the details will lead the client to their head and away from the essence of the gift metaphor. The quest is to experience and allow movement forward to come from the client only, with no direction coming from the Gestaltist. This assures that the client finds their *own* truth of the metaphor in the experiment.

Let's look at another example with a client named Jane.

"I feel as if I am hopelessly lost in a hot, sweltering jungle," Jane says. "I have a machete to clear a pathway by cutting through the trees and plant growth. I can hear someone behind me, but I only want to go forward."

Note: If the coach asks, "Is this jungle in Costa Rica or Africa?" the client goes to their mind, leaving the metaphor and thus halting the natural process altogether. If the coach tries to guide the client toward a solution, they might ask, "Is there a village you can see up ahead?" Again, this takes the power and ownership of this subconscious gift away from their client. And this eliminates any possibility for the client to make their own discovery.

However, in this case, what the coach says will not impede the process but support it.

"Stand up," the coach says. "Close your eyes. Feel the machete in your hand. See the jungle growth in front of you, blocking your pathway. Take a swipe to move forward."

By having the client actually step inside the metaphor, they move more into body somatics, and the metaphor comes alive. The client begins to cut the imaginary foliage and step slowly forward.

"What are you aware of now?" the coach asks.

"I need to get this cleared. I have to keep moving, even if it's hard," Jane replies.

"Keep cutting your way, and feel the sweltering heat as you do so. What are you aware of now?"

"There is someone behind me. I'm aware they are there, but I don't want to take the time to turn and look to see who it is."

"What emotions come up as you are aware that someone is there while you are clearing your way?"

"Fear."

"Stay with the fear. Allow yourself to feel it as you keep working with your machete."

Silence.

"I'm so hot, and this is so hard," Jane finally says. "I don't know how far I can do this. I'm not sure I can."

"What comes up for you as you are becoming aware that this may be too much for you?"

"The feeling of unsureness leaves, and I know I must keep going. I have no choice, and I want to cut harder and faster."

Jane moves forward, swinging the imaginary machete.

"Okay, so feel the jungle, the heat, the machete," the coach says. "Feel each cut and the pathway you are creating. And now?"

"Hmm. I don't think anyone is following me anymore. I don't feel them back there."

"And as you realize that, you feel . . .?"

"Relieved. Proud. I kept going, and I'm making my own way and creating my own way forward."

At some point, the metaphor begins to feel complete. This may be in two or three minutes or up to a half hour. It should not be rushed. The client emerges with their takeaway of new understandings and emotions around the situation the metaphor was expressing.

"So, quite a metaphor! What do you take away from experiencing it?" the coach asks.

"Wow! Well, I see now that the journey since my divorce has been hard. I've moved, made new friends, and found new ways to spend my time in my new city. I've begun to trust the choices I'm making in my new life. It's not been easy, and I'm proud of myself for not giving up."

The session continues.

Allowing the client's metaphor to expand without the coach guiding or changing it is an art form. It is letting go of all control of outcome. It is remembering that it is the client's metaphor. It's asking only questions that are based on the language the client has put forth. It takes focus on the part of the coach to allow the metaphor to expand.

For me, it is easier when I allow myself to imagine along with them and see, in my own mind's eye, the image they are creating. My body feels the fear or whatever emotion the client is feeling as the client is expressing it. I am walking along with them and remembering, at all times, that it's *their* metaphor. I'm an observer, and I'm careful not to change the meaning for the client. I don't want to alter a word that they're saying.

Do all of these experiments end positively? No. Some end in further turmoil. But given a bit more time, the human spirit finds a way to interpret the lesson or takeaway from the metaphor that is useful and adds understanding.

Working with metaphors might mean having the client close their eyes and remain seated, but when it is possible and when the metaphor is physical, I encourage the client to sit as they would inside a car or boat, on the back of a horse or a pink frog—whatever is presenting in the metaphor. If they are flying or standing in the image, I ask them to stand up and move as they are in the metaphor. Allowing the body to act out the metaphor adds subconscious information useful to the developing experience.

Whether brought forth in the natural dialogue between coach and client or created as an experiment in which the coach asks the client to describe the situation as a metaphor, we trust the process of the subconscious and its gifts of information to increase awareness.

15

Our Kaleidoscope

The human personality is comprised of many—maybe hundreds—of parts. Some are set in place in our DNA or come from traits that are similar between all biologically close relatives. Some are formed in response to our environment when we are growing up. Your family of origin, school-teachers, neighbors, babysitters, and others in your life have a hand in the formation of your personality and thus, your parts.

Some of our parts are formed from our temperament or typology, giving us clear preferences in terms of our learning style, social expression, and decision-making style, as well as how we use time and organize space. From our typology, many parts of self are created.

Other parts are formed from experiences unique to us, particularly those that teach us something about ourselves and those that are unfinished or leave scars and create our walls. Some of our parts form as we shift and change through the maturing process and take on different roles in life. We may move from sister and daughter to wife and mother, for example. Each role has its own needs, definitions, and understanding and serves to develop different parts of self to support them.

Parts form from conflicts, and they form from triumph. Each one is as unique to that person as their fingerprint. Two people can witness the same occurrence and see it differently.

Parts also develop from our values, which are formed during the maturation process. A person's values support their decisions and even lead to their identity. Some values are formed from positive experiences and impact what the person wants to move toward experiencing in life. Others are formed from emotional states that the person wants to avoid, or move away from. Each of these values contributes to the formation of many parts of self along the way, and all of our parts coexist in our personality. Each comes forth to run the show or to be in alignment to support other parts, either consciously or, more often, subconsciously. I see this process as the grand kaleidoscope of our personality.

Looking at the shards of glass in a kaleidoscope, we see it move to form and re-form a beautiful, if nonrepeatable, configuration and design. A miniscule shift or turn causes the pieces to slide and form an altogether new design. The same glass fragments are involved each time, but some move more into the forefront and others get covered up as they pattern together in a new way with each slight movement.

No part or shard is more important than any other, although some appear frequently and others rarely. We are whole when we recognize, honor, and own every part—the ones in the light and the ones in the shadow. There are no bad parts. Each formed for a specific reason, and each formed to assist the whole personality in some way.

Sometimes there are parts we would rather not have in charge or wish would be smaller because when they are present, they cause conflict or behavior that is not in our highest good or the good of others around us. But we still need to know those parts. We need to know why and how they formed and what they need from us now.

In our coaching, we work in the kaleidoscope concept, assisting the client in giving voice to their many parts and encouraging them to fully explore their parts and examine as many as we can find to see where and how they were formed and for what purpose they may have served. We work to understand and carry awareness of them, and we shine a light on the hidden parts and encourage them to have a voice.

There are many ways to work with a client's parts. An inventory may be taken by asking questions to form a mandala configuration to assist the client in actively working with and through the eyes of their many parts. In Gestalt experimentation, a dialogue between known parts can be creatively laid out to further and deepen insights about the parts and how they interact.

The coach might explore with their client which parts show up during conflict. This conglomerate of parts can be polar forces in the person taking opposing sides of the ring.

Let's say that the client knows that a part of themselves is open and patient, and yet, they are also aware that another part can be quick to form judgments. These two parts may be at opposite ends of the spectrum or in polarity to each other. When present for examination, these differing parts of self might have several statements of truth to say to each other, as well as appreciation for the circumstances in which they formed to begin with. These parts may have been formed when there was a need for protection, distraction, or defense, and now they perform when needed.

To become an integrated person with self-awareness, we study, examine, and know our parts. We know what triggers them to show up. We are aware when parts that will not aid the situation are present and how to release them from showing up in that moment.

We take responsibility for the role our parts play in each interaction with other people and their parts of self. The combination of parts and their formation directly impacts the multiple parts another person calls forth to interact.

In the example above, I may ask the client to sit in the awareness of the part of self that is open and patient. I ask her to explore what it feels like to be in that space and express from that place. Once a client has done work in this area, they are able to also identify other parts that come forth to support that part of self in interactions.

"Are you aware of any alliances of other parts of self?" I may ask.

The client may reply, "Yes. My 'think before speaking' and my 'good listener' parts are also backing up the 'open and patient' part."

"Good. Now sit on the other pillow and close your eyes. Feel into that part of you that you described as 'quick to form judgments.'"

She closes her eyes. "Yes, I feel that part."

"What else do you know about that part of self, how she formed in you, and what other shards are there in her alliance?"

"My impatient part and my critic are on board supporting this part, and 'quick to form judgments' feels a bit righteous or superior."

I then begin to facilitate a dialogue between these two major parts of self. Each expresses what they think of the other, what they feel when that part is running the show, or what awareness they hold of how differently they operate in situations. Often, one piece also unfolds into appreciation for the other.

There is never a time when a part is banished. All parts have formed for a reason, and it is an exercise in the importance of taking responsibility for when and how they show up. In the above example, it may play out as the "quick to judge" side expressing to the "open and patient" side by saying, "I appreciate that you help us explore opportunities that are important and can nurture relationships that develop into real depth and sincerity."

The "open and patient" side may respond, "And I thank you for times in our life when you have protected us from harm, based on our past trauma experiences as a child. When it feels familiar and our intuition is in doubt, you have moved us out of harm quickly. But because I'm an adult now, I ask you to hold off until I call upon you. I am willing to risk a bit of pain to explore new relationships."

This delicate negotiation between parts of self allows a dialogue that assists the client in forming conscious responsibility for how they interact with others. Gaining this personal awareness supports them when they move into a new group of peers. They can consciously use the model of entering with the "open and patient" part of self leading the way, trusting their ability to call forth their "quick to judge" and "critic" parts if needed.

Gestalt is rarely done with the client talking about something. Instead, all of the dialogue with these parts of self is directed by the coach between the parts. In this way, it becomes experiential, and the learning is integrated and useful in their life.

This compilation of parts usually exists outside our personal awareness. Through in-depth work in my Gestalt Coaching Method, this highly useful lens to view our interactions with others increases success in communication, management of emotions, and healthy relationships.

Carrying knowledge of our parts of self allows us to remain flexible in life. Conflicts become a dance of awareness about how the current formation of parts of self is reacting or responding to the other person in the situation. With awareness comes the opportunity to consciously pull up other parts of self, which then changes the dynamic dance. Both people adjust their parts of personality in every interaction, whether consciously or subconsciously. If they have awareness of self in this paradigm, they *choose* the parts coming forth instead of experiencing whatever comes forth unconsciously.

Conflicts can be both productive and unproductive. They are more healthy and creative interactions when the individuals in conflict are aware of and understand their parts of self and are able to consciously employ parts that are helpful in resolving the situation. We are less likely to be in a defensive mode or come from projection.

Our range of experience continues to grow throughout our lives. With that, new parts of self are formed and come aboard. Forming, acknowledging, and becoming familiar with all of our parts is a wondrous, long journey of self. And to the extent that a person understands how to explore and work with their parts using a healthy model, they will experience less polarity, both within themselves and in their interactions with others. While there may always be blind spots, Gestalt provides a medium for exploration in safety and in respect for the sacredness of self. When a polarity within arises, the person can explore it as they would if they were with an old friend, each stating their position with respect and honor as a part of their commitment to serve the relationship.

Let's look at another example in a coaching setting.

Jen is a recovering addict. She has been clean and sober for over a year now, and she is still paying close attention to her process. I ask her if she wants to explore the polarity within herself regarding her sobriety. She agrees.

I ask her to stand up, and I lay a rope in a line on the ground. "On which side of the pole does your sober side reside, and on which side does your addict side reside?"

She stops and thinks about it a second, then she points to one side. "That side is my sober side."

"Okay, stand on the sober side and move a bit while telling me who that Jen is. Think of yourself as a kaleidoscope or mandala with many parts that can come together to form aspects of yourself. What is the sober part of Jen like?"

"This is my serious side, my responsible side, and the healthy part of me," she replies.

"Now cross over to the other side of the rope and describe the addict part of yourself."

"This part of me is resistant and stubborn. It likes to avoid things."

"Okay," I say. "We're going to set up a dialogue between these two polarized parts of your being. Let's start with your addict self telling your sober self what you think about her, what your opinions of her are."

"Well, I mostly think you are great, but I also feel you are no fun."

She continues, and when the energy shifts, I ask her to switch sides and reply to sober's statements. We conduct a dialogue between the parts in this way until it feels complete.

This kind of experiment often takes about twenty minutes, and at the end of it, the person issues a heartfelt appreciation to both sides. The client has newfound clarity about the inner arguments that have been occurring outside her awareness. Done correctly, this is a revealing and supportive piece of work that allows for deep healing and expansion of awareness.

Every piece of work is creatively crafted by the coach to allow the client to fully explore their many parts and how and when they formed. Discovering and truly becoming acquainted with all the parts of our personality is key to Gestalt theory. A healthy self-concept is achieved by understanding and acknowledging the formation of these parts. Responsibility for actions, statements, and behaviors is achieved when a person has a full awareness and takes responsibility for making choices in the highest good of all parties. The kaleidoscope model identifies and gives voice to each part of self, allowing the person to continue to explore their uniqueness.

16

Wording, Senses, and Gestalt

Many of today's top methodologies for working with clients have roots deep in Gestalt. One that is popular due to its efficacy is the use of neuro-linguistic programming (NLP), which restructures the client toward the positive in the very functioning of the brain.

Much of the basic structure of NLP came from people observing and wanting to understand the results Fritz Perls was achieving in his seminal work. Often, it looked like magic, leading some theorists to break down his work to the choice of words he was using to achieve the desired result. Perls and his Gestalt theory formed a strong genesis for NLP theory thirty years before neuro-linguistic programming was founded in the 1970s.

As Perls developed his theory, he recognized words as giving an indication of the client's need to minimize or shift their awareness further away from their own experience. Our selection of words, both conscious and subconscious, tells an underlying story for the coach to become aware of in the work with their client. As I work with clients, I am interested in their choice of words when they are describing an event or an emotion. For instance, a client who moves the impact of their statement away from themselves might sound like the following.

"How do you feel about this situation?" I ask.

A client attempting to remove responsibility from themselves for the situation might reply, "Well, when this happens you feel . . ."

I then encourage them to repeat their statement using the pronoun *I* so they can own the comment and the feelings attached to it.

I also encourage my students to be alert for when the client uses the pronoun *it.* If the client says, "It makes me angry," the coach might say, "Look inside. When you say *it,* who or what do you mean by that word?"

"Oh, my dad. My dad makes me angry. He drinks too much at dinner," the client may reply.

Using the pronoun *it* can be used to keep the statement emotionally distanced from the client. It is important for the client to speak their own truth and stand in awareness of how they truly feel.

Further correction is often warranted as the client uses the phrase *makes me feel.* This phrase is completely integrated into our culture through television and our social way of connecting. However, it implies that the person has neither a sense of their own feelings nor a sense of personal control. Asking "How does it make you feel?" is the epitome of language used to shield the person from taking responsibility in the exchange. A soft but clear correction when this is stated is "How do you feel when this occurs?" or "What feelings are you aware of when this happens in your life?"

This removal of ownership can happen even when we make positive statements that remove ourselves from what we are saying, depersonalizing the statement. If I say, "Green eyes are so attractive," instead of, "I am attracted to your green eyes, Dane," I am removing ownership of my words and feelings.

Learning how to make these language adjustments assists a person in self-awareness and in developing a more authentic self. The adjustment of the very *choice* of words also guides the mind toward change, in part because internal dialogue describes pictures, feelings, sounds, smells, and tastes. Gestalt recognizes that becoming self-aware of word choice, gestures, facial expressions, and parts of self, aids a person in stopping projections and seeing what is really there instead of imagining it or making it up.

As a Gestalt coach, you remain observant of all clues the client shares. The body's signals and person's behaviors align, providing clues about the transmissions between the conscious, subconscious, and even the unconscious mind. Sensory awareness and the focus on sensory-based work came from Perls, who often led an exercise encouraging the client to complete the stem "Now I am aware." This exercise expanded the client's awareness of their five primary senses. Often, he would add in his infamous joke, "The patient must lose their mind and come to their senses!"

In his early Gestalt experiments in the 1950s, Perls asked clients to express themselves through their visual sense

("What do you see?"), their auditory sense ("How does that sound to you?"), or their kinesthetic sense ("How solid does that seem?"). These align with today's modern understanding of NLP, as well as NLP's VAK (visual, auditory, kinesthetic) model that explores predicate phrases.

If a person uses words such as *look, appears, enlighten, foresee,* or *scope* in their speaking, they may be more visually attuned to the world around them. Auditorily aligned people may say the words *echo, babble, buzz, grumbling,* and *screech* when describing their world. And if a person leans more to the kinesthetic, they will select words such as *hold, bounce, press, dig in,* or *clutch* to express themselves.

Understanding the client's preference may assist the coach in building rapport when in contact with their client. This may be done by matching or shifting their own way of self-expression to the major field the client is speaking from. Remaining cognizant of their patterns of speech, speed, and syntax, as well as their body language, can give clues in building rapport with the client.

Further, I personally experience that most clients believe our senses are limited to the five physical ones of sight, sound, smell, taste, and touch. This is another limiting belief established as early as first grade in elementary school. In our educational system, children are given the introject from their teacher's curriculum that we have only five senses.

A six-year-old child is quite happy and proud to learn this seemingly important lesson, which is often on one of their first quizzes in school. If they answer *five* and can name them, they receive a gold star on their quiz paper. Thus, a belief is established that we have only five senses when, in fact, more and more people today are aware that we have many, many senses that serve us by bringing credible information.

Using my intuition and field of awareness that runs far beyond the basic physical senses adds to the creativity of the work. This also allows for greater expression of information from the client because they are given permission to trust their inner knowing and inexplicable understanding of their life.

Often, when sitting in front of a client and beginning to find true contact with them, I experience an empathic response. My body is a tuned instrument, and before taking my place with the client, I have quickly scanned how my own body feels—heart, breathing, gut, etc. In that way, I can open up as a blank slate to feeling what the client is actually feeling in their body. Commonly, I feel my stomach tighten, my neck become tense, or a headache form before the client begins to put into words the physical symptoms they are experiencing. Using my own body as an open instrument, what the client is feeling—often an imploded state—becomes apparent to me. If they fail to express their body sensations, I will trust my own and use the information to explore if they are imploded at that place or chakra point. Often, once discussed, the symptoms go away.

Perhaps an example here might help. Donna was the last person to work with me in group one night. She was a new member and had been observing the Gestalt work for two hours before seeking to do her own work with me. As we sat across from one another, I felt centered and then became extremely short of breath. Having never experienced difficulties with my lungs, I trusted that my shortness of breath was a message from my body about Donna's process.

"Do you have asthma?" I asked.

Another way in which my intuition serves me is a personal rule I follow to not ask for any information about a client who comes to me. My appointments are handled by one of my assistants. I only know their first name and the time of the appointment. I have no information based on any discussion they might have had with my assistant. I prefer to go into the session in the present moment and allow the work to emerge. My intuitive awareness, however, will act as an accurate guide for where to begin to explore. Sometimes I even have a sentient understanding of part of the client's life that they have not verbalized. They will give me a strange look and ask how I know something. I'm honest and say that it just came to me.

A rather dramatic example of this once happened with a family of four. The mother introduced her two children and husband, saying that her husband of three years was the boys' stepfather and had adopted them. I replied, "Oh, did this occur after the house fire?" The mom gasped and asked how I knew about the fire. I told her I really didn't know but that the image of a fire had come to me. Before the session, I did not even know their names, but as I sat with them, I felt their sadness and saw the fire.

I believe everyone has these abilities and even work with my students to heighten and further develop their own. The introjections that people do not have these abilities or that they are extra or odd serves only to block people from their natural abilities. I choose to accept them and have always given myself permission to open into my full senses. These experiences are commonplace for me in my work.

In Gestalt, we look less at what is being said and more at the "how" of the expressed comment or story. The story is the client's memory of their own unfinished business. It is personal to them. We are not looking at absolute truth. We are looking at how it is programmed in the client's viewpoint because how their subconscious holds the information is their truth.

If there are four children in a family and all of them remember a traumatic incident, they will each see it differently. It is the same event, but each has gathered it in uniquely through their temperament, developmental age, values, and relationship to the people involved. Gestalt looks at the pattern. While sitting across from the client, the coach is trusting the process that the client's perception is their own viewpoint. It may not be the absolute truth, but it is their own truth as they see it. And neuro-linguistics expresses the sub-context, yielding clues for the coach to pursue in setting up the work.

In Gestalt, we do not ask a client *why*, and we also encourage our clients to stop asking that question. Therapy oriented to discussing the past is invalid because in asking why, the practitioner receives an answer filtered through the patient's neurosis, and it will rarely explain anything that leads to healing. Asking why opens up to more questions and puts the client in their head without all of the information needed. The information needed actually comes with personal awareness of their body, their viewpoint, and their whole self. Asking why produces pat answers, rationalizations, excuses, and delusions with regard to an event, as if it could be explained by a single answer.

Rather than asking why, Gestaltists ask *how*. When the experiments are completed and the unfinished business is completed, the client sees clearly and will automatically have their own answers. A healthy person may still have parts of self or use language outside their awareness. They are healthy enough to continue to explore and learn more about themselves. Disturbed individuals lack awareness and have large, gaping holes in their understanding of self. Linguistics can be a helpful road map to lead us to clarity.

NLP focuses on linguistic distinctions. Again, from Perls's original work in Gestalt, there are many examples of sessions and pieces of work with clients during which a client would make a statement like "I must do this." Perls would challenge the word *must*. He would ask who was supplying the must and explore with the client what would really happen if they didn't do whatever it was that they believed they must do. He challenged the meta words, like *should, must,* and *always.* He believed that the neurosis and anxiety people feel from outside pressures come from their use of the meta-globalizing words they use when defining their experiences. Years later, NLP tied this concept up neatly in what is called the meta-model of linguistics.

What we recognize today is that language affects results. The words we choose are very important for both the speaker and the receiver. Language comes from both a conscious and a subconscious place, and often, it is coming more from the subconscious than the conscious. The body adds to the language and reinforces or negates what the speaker is attempting to convey. If we are not specific or use language that keeps our pain at bay, this needs to be recognized by the coach so they can assist the client in full ownership of their self-expression and feelings.

As clients move through their journey of awareness with a Gestaltist, they make several small and subtle changes en route to becoming an individual who says what they mean and means what they say. The words are accompanied with full awareness of their own authentic voice and hold the ring of their truth.

17

Bringing Horses Into My Work

I have been a horsewoman since I was ten years old and have had hundreds of horses in my care during my life. I have partnered with horses in traditional ways, but I have also been one of the earliest pioneers in working with them to emotionally heal humans.

I've owned several ranches and boarding facilities while raising horses, training them, and showing them in competition. I've had the unique experience of breeding and raising horses at a top level as well as trail riding all over the United States. I share all of this as a small glimpse into the depth of my traditional experience with equines.

In the 1980s, I bought a small twenty-five-acre ranch with my husband (now ex-husband) as a summer refuge for our family to escape the desert heat of our Cave Creek, Arizona, ranch. The new ranch bordered the Coconino Forest in Flagstaff, Arizona. I escaped with our children as soon as school let out and usually hauled eight or so horses up there with us. My husband commuted up for a weekend whenever his work allowed. I continued to see clients there and did several retreats.

One summer I began to notice that the horses were interacting on their own with my clients when they were on break between sessions. What I witnessed was that it seemed far easier for my clients to access and express deep emotions after they had been in the presence of horses. They would often self-report a profound feeling in their body while standing in the presence of the horse. The internet was not yet invented, so I could not compare notes with any therapists.

By the following summer, I began inviting my clients to join me at the barn and purposefully created Gestalt Contact between a horse and my client. That same summer, I experimented with having the horse observe the full Gestalt sessions through a round pen fence and eventually crafted the Equine Gestalt Coaching (EGC) Method I use and teach today.

As the internet came online, I knew I was the first—and most likely only—person combining Gestalt with equines in a professional way. By the 2000s, there were a few others who had adopted the concept in their own style. At Touched by a Horse, I had the advantage of having two hundred highly trained and skilled Certified Equine Gestalt Coaching Method coaches around the world using my proven method. In 2018, we released a scientific study involving eight EGC practitioners and over 180 clients that describes the true, proven efficacy of our method.

Horses are natural Gestaltists. They hold no judgments and live in the present moment in their daily lives. They are keenly aware and expressive of their somatic energy fields and are highly self-aware of who they are, so they show up honestly when interacting with each other or a person. They desire for humans to clean up their energy fields and not hold on to anger or emotions that are making them ill.

Contrasted to dogs, who chum easily and do tricks for a food treat, horses are in the prey side of the predator-prey polarity. They seek authenticity and congruence to feel safe. This means that they have a keen, natural ability to reveal when they sense a person who is thinking, feeling, and intuiting their personal truth as well as someone who is lying to themselves or thinking one way and feeling another.

In our EGC Method, horses are seen as our partners—a second coach in the session. Each horse has their own unique gifts and way of expressing their clairsentient awareness to the Gestalt Coach. They are keenly drawn to the authenticity of the Gestalt experiments, sensitive to the contact cycle and the authenticity required of the clients. The horses are full-on partners in the process. This is not a system in which we anthropomorphize onto the horse, nor do they simply participate during the debriefing process after an activity, as is common in the equine-assisted healing field. In our unique method of combining the experiential nature of Gestalt and the pieces of work in the presence of the horse, they become free to express what they notice, see, and feel energetically with our clients.

People who are unfamiliar with horses may be somewhat taken aback by this concept. But for me, it is an example of how humans feel superior to animals in our abilities to think and feel. In actuality, many animals have proven that they are brilliant in their own right and often in areas we don't understand and therefore deny. I don't deny. My horses are brilliant in the Equine Gestalt Coaching Method work, and I am honored and very blessed that they showed themselves to me in this way over thirty years ago.

Today, I work as a human who can assist horses in expressing their healing gifts, and I honor them for the true healers they are.

18

A Way of Life

I feel very fortunate to have found a talented Gestalt therapist when I made my first attempt at getting personal therapy. Gestalt became an important part of my own journey. I worked with many talented Gestalt practitioners, both for my personal healing and later as a trainee, before becoming a Gestalt therapist and coach. I healed my personal unfinished business and wounds and later worked professionally as a Gestaltist with others. Hundreds—perhaps even thousands—of clients have come through my door or entered my arena. And I am always honored to sit with them and explore who they have become and the *how* of their life.

One of the experiences I am not sure I would have survived without Gestalt was the twenty-five-year journey of raising my daughter, who was always dancing on the razor's edge of life and death.

It was because I had embodied Gestalt that I was able to help her stay in each moment and not become anxious to know the outcome of the many challenges she faced. And I was able to take personal responsibility for how I was feeling on the journey with all the many attitudes and personalities we faced along the way.

I did not ask myself why. And I never heard my daughter do so either. We asked a Gestalt how. We stayed present, up until and through her passing. We did not allow unfinished business to be created as we moved through it all. I'm eternally grateful to have held Gestalt as my personal pathway to understanding and feeling every step of the way, so there are no regrets.

Horses have always been my most trusted confidants in life. In my young adulthood, when I was training in Gestalt, I began to see what supreme, embodied Gestaltists horses are in their own right. They never ask why. They live in the present moment. They are not interested in what we think, and they are highly tuned in to how we feel. They have deep somatic understanding and can read the human body on several energy levels. All of this and much more became my pathway to designing my Equine Gestalt Coaching Method. There are two Gestaltists present with the client—one human and one equine. As my equine partners see that which is fragmented become whole alongside the coach, the peace flows through all of us—coach, horse, and client.

Becoming a Gestalt trainer in different capacities has been a rewarding career. Along the way, forming my own method based in Gestalt and incorporating many other modalities mentioned in this book, I trademarked the Equine Gestalt Coaching Method and the Gestalt Coaching Method. In both of these methods, I have combined Co-Active Coaching, NLP, chakra work, typology, body language, psychodrama, and other alchemical modalities with Gestalt to achieve highly effective healing.

When working with a group or a couple, I find that there is a phenomenon commonly experienced that I have come to call *borrowed benefit*. As humans, we are both unique and similar to others at the same time. One person's traumatic experience, when worked on in a vulnerable state, assists healing and understanding in many who observe the work.

As I have continued to allow life to open and soften my heart, my consciousness has also formed many gradations of awareness that serve me well as a practitioner. As my spiritual self has expanded, I have found living life in the present moment as my core experience. I have observed that this is at the center of all spiritual teachings on the earth. For me to love and share love lies at the core of my work.

Not long ago, an interviewer asked me if there was a common denominator to all my work, since it all looked so creative and different to her. I thought and responded that assuredly, it is always to assist the person in finding self-compassion and peace.

We grow up having unique experiences in our families of origin, but as adults, we forget that we were not always mature adults when many of these things were happening to and around us. Often, we survive and move on in our lives without taking inventory of all we have been through. As we move on and begin to create and experience our lives, the places where we become stuck, confused, or hurt trigger the unfinished state. Some people find a desire to live a better emotional life and know what makes them tick.

As the discovery roads lead back to the unfinished bits, clients are often surprised, as I was in my own work, by how young they were when the unfinished business was created. They might have actually been only seven years old and powerless to impact what was happening, or they might have been a teen without the skill set to deal with aggression. As they begin to awaken to the truth of where they were at that age and what was possible, they can begin to feel compassion for their inner self and view themselves with love and understanding. The work is never about self-pity. Self-compassion is a state of truth felt through love, and it truly heals the soul.

These inner shifts to awareness and wholeness in my own journey have not happened overnight. I have learned from my students and clients over the decades and value their presence in my life. The parts of self I identify in my being today are vast and varied, each formed in response to the life and experiences I have endured and created. Remembering that precious life is in fact in session, it is always my desire to remain open and curious about where I am presently so that I may savor my life.

Remaining resourceful, kind, passionate, accomplished, grateful, nurturing, loving, and generous are the keys for me to follow my number one value in my life: to make a difference. I am driven by that value statement and express it in small acts, as well as in daily practice, to stay in balance. By serving others who are seeking growth and enjoying the process, I can do so with love and gratitude for myself and others.

To work with others by providing a container of safety in which they feel free to take a deep breath, courageously explore, drink from the pool of wholeness, and experience love of self while releasing the critical voice is my calling.

As a Gestaltist, I will continue to midwife souls as long as I am allowed to on this planet.

Gestalt Quiz

How does the cover photo relate to Gestalt?

This is an example of foreground/background.
Find the hidden faces.

Acknowledgments

Gestalt is the framework of my life. It is complex and usually taught and written about in a manner of great intellectualization. My intent with this book is to bring a complex subject matter to a more user-friendly level that invites readers from all walks of life to form a better understanding of the key principles. In this way, they may benefit personally from Gestalt.

I honor all of my Gestalt teachers and other authors of Gestalt, whom I respectfully ask to receive my interpretation and field view of Gestalt. I have taken certain liberties and expanded Gestalt theory and shared it in this book. My thirty-five years of private practice and more than sixteen years of teaching these concepts have undoubtedly evolved my personal understanding and application of theory.

I have many people to thank for their support and feedback in the writing and publication of this book. At the beginning of the writing process, I sent email copies of the manuscript to my freshman and junior certification students. Thank you to those who read and responded to that email. I feel certain you will not recognize the finished book, and I thank you for your feedback and assistance in the process. Alongside these students, I selected certain graduates of our programs for the same purpose. Thank you. With experience under your belt, your feedback helped me home in on the most important topics.

I am grateful to several contributors to the book's illustrative content. Sharon MacNaughton, your printing of charts allowed me to illustrate a complex view of the energy cycle in the manner I have within the book. Thank you for your artistic talent. Alice Griffin, your clever illustrations throughout the book have brought one of my key principles to life: to have fun while learning. We are meant to learn through joy and creativity, and your drawings have certainly brought life to the subject. Thank you.

Certified Practitioner Mara Greve from Latvia, I thank you for allowing me to incorporate your homework in this book. It aids in understanding the breaks in the energy cycle beautifully. Mara, you are a deep, thoughtful, and brilliant person, and I am grateful for your participation.

I am not a careful typist because my mind lopes ahead of my ability to type. I'm talented at expressing myself in lecture, but I did not pay attention well enough in English class. Therefore, I'm sending a huge thank you and deep bow of gratitude to Peggy MacArthur, who received each rough draft and polished it enough for my editor to receive. Peggy, your knowledgeable feedback, proofer's eye, support, friendship, and encouragement have made this book project possible.

Our cover shot is a photo by Kim Beer. Kim, I asked for an equine picture that would help me represent the Gestalt principle foreground/background, and you had it in your archives! Thank you for your consistent support of my projects through your vast talents. Once again, our collaboration has brought forth a fun cover.

Until I became a writer, I had no real concept of what an important job the editor holds. Now, after several book projects, I am clear that my editor, Melanie Mulhall, like a good ranch manager, is central in producing a readable, coherent, and finished book! In some parts, a trencher was needed. In others, a plow. Still other parts required a herding dog or watering can to manage the project. Melanie, alongside the team of professionals you have led me to, thank you once again for helping me plant and grow this labor of love into a book.

To my staff, Risa, Jessica, and Jen, thank you for keeping the place running smoothly while I locked myself away writing.

And to my husband, Dane, thank you for your love and laughter and sweet breaks from writing that source me fully. My "contact" with you allows each present moment to be rich.

About the Author

Melisa Pearce is the founder of Touched by a Horse® and the creator of the Equine Gestalt Coaching Method® and the Gestalt Coaching Method®. Her passion and life's work as a healer, mentor, and teacher have encompassed Gestalt from the beginning. Melisa Pearce is a lifelong horsewoman, therapist, coach, and entrepreneur. Much of her professional success has come through her understanding and dedication to Gestalt practices and methodologies.

Melisa has been a psychotherapist, master coach, Gestaltist, and author for more than thirty years. Over the last three decades, she has coached and helped others through her private psychotherapy practice and partnership with horses. She developed her unique method of combining Gestalt with her horses in Gestalt sessions beginning in the 1980s.

This partnership with horses led her to create the Equine Gestalt Coaching Method®, a therapeutic approach to deep-process emotional healing through the exploration of self, based in Gestalt. Many times this methodology incorporates an equine partner as a co-equal coach. As of early 2019, there are close to two hundred certified EGCM practitioners worldwide from countries as far away as South Africa and Singapore. These graduates, along with their equine partners, help their clients find positive futures through the EGCM methodology.

Melisa Pearce is the author of the inspirational card deck *Whispers from a Horse's Heart* and the novel *Eponalisa*. She has coauthored several books, including *Games People Play with Horses* and *Equusology*.

In the award-winning book *Equusology*, she explores human and horse typology and the art of human-equine relationship. As editor, Melisa Pearce recently released the third book in the anthology series entitled *Touched by a Horse, Equine Coaching Stories*. These consecutive volumes feature stories of hope and healing written by the certified graduates and students of the Touched by a Horse Equine Gestalt Coaching Method®.

Melisa lives on her ranch near Elizabeth, Colorado, with her husband Dane Cheek, her herd of equine partners, and a veritable menagerie of animals.

Want More of Melisa Pearce and Touched by a Horse®?

Equine Gestalt Coaching Method® Certification Program

Melisa Pearce has applied her mastery of the Gestalt concepts shared in this book with her decades of groundbreaking work with horses as healers to create the Touched by a Horse® Equine Gestalt Coaching Method® (EGCMethod) Certification Program. Applicants do not need previous horse experience to start a successful career partnering with horses using the EGCMethod. More information can be found on **http://www.TouchedbyaHorse.com** or by calling Touched by a Horse at **866-652-8704**.

Keynote Speaking and Personal Appearances

Melisa Pearce is a master communicator. Her success in translating human behavior through observation and interaction with horses has made her a highly effective speaker. Melisa is able to tailor her comments to her audience whether it is in an arena, auditorium, personal retreat setting, or a business/sales team meeting. She provides keynote addresses, workshops, live video streaming, and webinars. If you are interested in inviting Melisa to speak or teach at your event, please email **office@TouchedbyaHorse.com** for more information or call Touched by a Horse at **866-652-8704**.

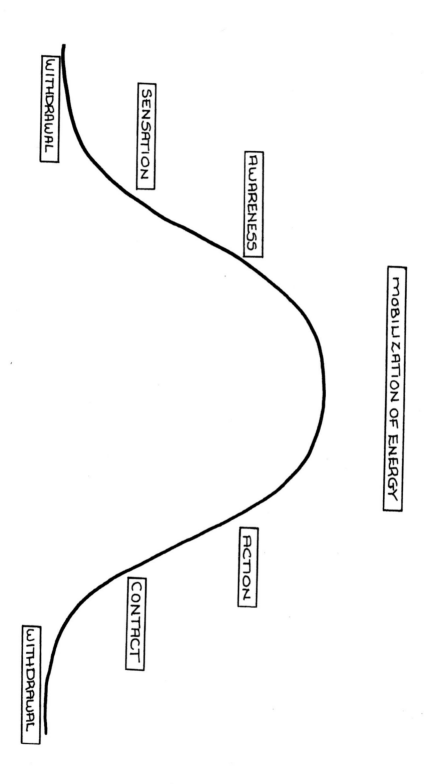